The World of
JAZZ

The World of
JAZZ

In printed ephemera and collectibles

Jim Godbolt

WELLFLEET
PRESS

The World of Jazz
Published 1990 by The Wellfleet Press
A Division of Book Sales, Inc.
110 Enterprise Avenue, Secaucus
New Jersey 07094, USA

First published 1990 by Studio Editions Ltd.
Princess House, 50 Eastcastle Street
London W1N 7AP, England.

ISBN 1-55521-623-4

Printed and bound in Czechoslovakia

Publishers Note: Every effort has been made to locate
and credit copyright holders of material reproduced in
this book, and they apologise for any omissions.

Contents

Introduction
6

New Orleans: Land of Dreams
8

The First Recordings
22

The First of the Big Bands
40

Jazz Crosses the Atlantic
54

Swing Fever
76

Jazz Consolidates in Britain
88

Back to the Roots
102

The Bebop Revolution
118

A Rich Tapestry
136

Bibliography
157

Index
158

Acknowledgements
160

May 26

Melody Maker

MAY 26, 1956 — **EVERY FRIDAY 6d.**

Donegan in U.S
Report on page 4

'JUNGLE MUSIC' CRY AT RANDALL U.S SHOW

GOLD DISCS FOR WINNIE

New York, Monday.

THE White Citizens Council of Birmingham, Alabama—who were responsible for the attack on Nat "King" Cole during Ted Heath's concerts there—again caused trouble when Freddy Randall appeared at the Civic Auditorium.

The Randall band, in a package including "Rock 'n Roll" king Bill Haley and his Comets played before a segregated audience at the Auditorium on Sunday.

Council pickets paraded outside the hall carrying printed signs reading "Down with bebop. Christians will not attend this show. Ask your preacher about jungle music!"

Teenagers hit back

The pickets were in turn picketed by teenagers who shouted "Rock 'n Roll is here to stay!"

The White Citizens Council, in condemning the craze, have linked "Rock 'n Roll" with sin, degradation and Communism.

The band is booked for 16 towns in Louisiana, Alabama, Tennessee, South Carolina, North Carolina, Georgia, Florida, Virginia and at the best small Guard Armouries available.

This means that Randall, like Ted Heath, will get a very untypical view of America, playing many of the same Jim Crow theatres and auditoriums. But his permit has been extended to

Back Page, Col. 2

ified Atwell, currently at
London Palladium, was
ecialists — Pilip-Co — with
gold ruments — in turn a
rman. Philips Records. They
were in recognition of the
fact that two of her records,
"Let's Have A Party" and
"Let's Have Another Party,"
on the Philips label, have
each sold over a million
copies. Her Decca "Black
and White Rag" is also approaching a million sales.

Stephane Grappelly arriving from Paris for TV

SWING violinist Stephane Grappelly arrives from Paris tomorrow (Saturday) to guest in ATV's "Jack Jackson Show" on Sunday and in BBC-TV's "Tin Pan Alley Show" the following day.

Stephane has been appearing at the Claridge Hotel and Club St. Germain in Paris.

Also starring in the "Tin Pan Alley Show" are Ronnie Hilton, the Ken-Tones vocal group and Shani Wallis. The concert orchestra is conducted by Stanley Black.

Stephane will also air in "British Jazz" over the BBC on June 1.

ROLLINI TRIBUTE ON THE AIR

JAZZ writer and record collector Brian Rust will present a memorial programme on Adrian Rollini, who died last week, in the BBC Light programme's "World of Jazz" on June 8.

Adrian's brother, Arthur Rollini—who played tenor with Benny Goodman in the 1930s—is trying to solve the mystery surrounding Adrian's death.

Bass saxist and vibist Adrian was found in Florida lying in a blood-spattered car. One of his feet was almost severed. He died in hospital on May 15 after a heart attack and lung collapse.

Comparatively wealthy, Adrian had been out of the jazz scene for many years.

Satchmo's farewell

Louis Armstrong and his wife Lucille left London Airport on Tuesday for Accra to a fanfare played on a toy trumpet by Lucille. The trumpet was presented to Louis by the Commissioner for the Gold Coast. Louis, who will play to an estimated audience of 30,000 Africans on the Gold Coast, is due back in New York tomorrow (Saturday). (Story: Back Page.)

Dizzy flies in as Louis leaves Britain

TWO and a half hours after Louis Armstrong and his All Stars left London Airport on Tuesday for the Gold Coast, Dizzy Gillespie flew in with his big band.

The Gillespie Orchestra had flown from Athens, where it had just completed an eight-week U.S. State Department-sponsored tour of the Far East, Middle East, Yugoslavia and Greece.

With Dizzy were arranger and trumpet player Quincy Jones, the band's MD; Carl Warwick, Ermet Perry and Joe Gordon (tpts.); Frank Rehak, Rod Levitt and Melba Liston (the girl trombonist and arranger) (tmbs.); Phil Woods and Jimmy Powell (altos); Ernie Wilkins and Billy Mitchell (tnrs.); Marty Flax (bari.), Walter Davis (pno.); Nelson Boyd (bass) and Charles Persip (drs.).

This was Gillespie's first visit to Britain since he came over with Teddy Hill's orchestra in 1937.

In a brief interview at the airport, Dizzy told the MM: "The tour has been a great success—

Back Page, Col. 5

STATES TRIP PLANS FOR DANKWORTH

New York, Wednesday.—Johnny Dankworth is the latest British bandleader under consideration for an American tour.

Subject to suitable union arrangements, he will bring his group here for a series of concert dates in late October or early November.

BRITISH JAZZMEN IN CHAPLIN FILM

AN all-star British jazz group, which contains five bandleaders, will appear in the new Charlie Chaplin film, A King In New York, which is currently being shot at Shepperton Studios.

The bandleaders are saxist Dave Shand, trombonist Bobby Mickleburgh, tenorist Tubby Hayes, drummer Tony Crombie and pianist Norman Long.

The personnel will be completed by bassist Ronnie Seabrook and Alan Wickham, trumpeter with the newly formed Bobby Mickleburgh Band.

The film, a comedy, stars Chaplin with Shani Wallis, Dawn Addams and Joy Nichols.

The band will be heard and seen playing in a night club sequence.

Erroll Garner in taxi accident

New York, Wednesday.—Erroll Garner is in the Lenox Hill Hospital with concussion and a possible blood clot following a taxi accident in New York.

Another cab crashed into the back of his own and Erroll was badly shaken up.

Martha Glaser, his manager, suffered an injured back but is stated to be recovering.

Introduction

Although specific dates are debatable, jazz is now generally agreed to be about a hundred years old. Although its early beginnings just before the turn of the century are of necessity partly a matter of conjecture, a massive weight of historical detail and memorabilia has since been accumulated concerning the music, musicians, performances and recordings that make up the jazz movement.

Jazz is multi-faceted, and each facet could easily merit a separate volume of its own. The intention of this book is to evoke the stages of jazz's development in words and contemporary ephemera, to outline the major events, to describe the more significant – and a few of the minor – figures, and to reproduce just some of the vast collection of visual memorabilia that is part of jazz's pictorial history.

While it was unfortunate that the early jazz pioneers were not recorded on gramophone record for posterity's judgement, mercifully the camera had been invented in time to capture many valuable images of the musicians that, by showing the instrumentation and some of the surroundings of the players, give visual substance to the recollections and written historical details of the period.

The extraordinary number of recording companies in the 1920s has meant that a large number of highly attractive labels still exist, of which a representative selection is included in this book. The introduction of the long-playing record in the early 1950s – which saw the demise of the 78rpm record – provided yet another avenue for artistes to exercise their imagination in the production of album covers, noteworthy examples of which are those by David Stone Martin for the 'Jazz at the Philharmonic' issues. The reader is advised to make the most of these covers, for the LP album will probably soon join the cylinder and 78rpm record as a thing of the past, with record companies increasingly going over to compact disc. Many early album covers are pictured here, for their visual interest and for their historical significance.

Overall, the aim of the book has been to evoke and reflect the progression of jazz over the last century, reflecting not only the music but the social and racial mores that attended its history. In this regard some of the material relating to the stereotype of the black performer (a stereotype often encouraged at the time by the artistes themselves) will now appear to be offensive, but to exclude such material would be to deny the important racial elements of jazz's social and historical development.

Left: A superb piece of ephemera which illustrates exactly why the collection of such memorabilia can be so fascinating and worthwhile. On a single front page of Britain's *Melody Maker* (20th May 1956) there are over ten separate items or features which serve to encapsulate the attitudes of the day, and to document them in a way that cannot be distorted by the passing of time. Ephemera adds a sense of colour and a touch of humour – as well as an atmosphere of immediacy – to the study of jazz history which pure academic analysis will never match.

Canal Street

New Orleans: Land of Dreams

Won't you come along with me
Down the Mississippi
We'll take the boat to the land of dreams
Steam down the river, down to New Orleans

(The first stanza of 'Basin Street Blues',
a song commemorating one of the most
famous of New Orleans' streets.)

'A fantastic and wonderful city. A city with a hundred faces. The hard face for commerce and the soft face for making love. Scratching figures on the back of an envelope where the girl with the deep dark eyes waits on counter. Smell of burnt coffee and sound of ships. The deep face for a sad life and the pinched face for poverty. Marching, singing, laughing. The silver and copper laugh of the prostitute, and the toothless chuckle of the old man who remembers Buddy Bolden at Bogalusa.

Every writer makes his own city. The city of fine living and free spirit, woven into the dream of a poet. The city of brass bands and military marches, grand balls and rowdy lakefront parties. The city of Lulu White and Mahogany Hall, Josie Arlington and the palm tree growing crazily there in a vacant lot. The thin young man who drinks too much, looking at Congo Square, squeezing the last acrid sweetness out of sight and sound.

'Come on and hear
Come on and hear'

This is our city, not so far from Madame John's legacy but carrying with it another legacy, the dark human cargo of a Yankee slaver, the Marquis de Vaudreuil, raising a thin glass above a fringed cuff, drinking the drink and shattering the glass into tiny tinkling fragments. Bamboula and tinkling glass. Flat voices of invitation behind shuttered cribs. Canal Street murky yellow with night, her standards the Carnival colors, symbols of transient ownership, like a mistress smiling in turn at her lovers.

Up Rampart beyond Canal. That's Uptown. That's Bolden territory. Perdido by the gas works. Maybe there used to be a cypress swamp there but nobody remembers now. Everybody remembers Bolden and his barber shop and his scandal sheet and his ragtime band, playing a new music that didn't have a name of its own. (They say the word for it came from Chicago "down around 22nd"; they say it came from an Elizabethan slang word meaning hit it hard and from an American slang word meaning it don't mean a thing but it costs real money around 22nd.)

Don't look for the eagle on the Eagle Saloon. And don't look for Masonic Hall because it's a vacant lot. But listen hard some night, listen hard at the corner of Rampart and Perdido and you'll hear a whacky horn playing an Uptown rag, way out and way off, filling out the tune. That would be King Bolden, calling his children.'

The above is part of the introduction to *Jazzmen* by Frederic Ramsey Jnr. and Charles Edward Smith.

General Note: Throughout the book, the names in the captions to pictures containing groups of characters are listed left to right.

Top left: Canal Street, New Orleans. **Far left:** Lulu White's Mahogany Hall. This was one of New Orleans' notorious 'sporting houses'. Situated in the area, Storyville, which was officially designated as the red light district, it provided employment for many musicians, mostly 'piano professors', such as Ferdinand 'Jelly Roll' Morton. Miss White's establishment was situated on the corner of Basin and Bienville Streets, and aside from her 'handsome' women, her mansion contained some of the most valuable oil paintings in the South. A special feature of the interior decoration was the large number of gaudily ornate mirrors – on the ceilings as well as the walls. **Left:** Buddy Bolden's Band, c.1894. Standing: Frank Lewis, clarinet; Willie Cornish, valve trombone; Buddy Bolden, trumpet; Jimmy Johnson, bass. Seated: Willie Warner, clarinet; Brock Mumford, guitar. Buddy Bolden is one of the legendary figures of New Orleans jazz, and it was said that his playing was so powerful that it could be heard 14 miles away on a clear night. He is alleged to have made a cylinder recording, but as it has never been found there is no certainty about the sound produced by what was primarily a marching band.

Above: The Woodland Band, 1905. Edward Robinson, banjo; Kid Ory, valve trombone; Chif Matthews, trumpet; Raymond Brown, violin; Stonewall Matthews, guitar; Harry Forster, string bass (which provides a convenient peg for his hat). This was Kid Ory's first band, and is pictured here at La Place, Louisiana, his birthplace. Ory achieved fame among collectors for his contribution to the historic Hot Five and Hot Seven recordings made by Louis Armstrong in the 1920s. He was one of the many musicians who enjoyed a totally unexpected upsurge in his fortunes thanks to the New Orleans Renaissance that started in the mid-1940s.

Right: Buddy Bolden's home. Bolden was born on 6th September 1877, one of many great jazzmen to come from very humble surroundings. According to legend, heavy drinking and womanizing contributed to his relatively early demise in an insane asylum on 4th November 1931.

Jazzmen was a romantic vision of a city whose contribution to American music Ramsey and Smith researched in the late 1930s. The book contains many inaccuracies (it has been established, for example, that Buddy Bolden never had a barber's shop or published a scandal sheet) but *Jazzmen*'s romantic approach was excusable considering that up to that time the city that spawned jazz had been almost totally overlooked by jazz writers and enthusiasts, as other, more publicly acceptable, developments in the North stole the limelight. It was the first book to establish the historical importance of New Orleans jazz and included some moving correspondence from those there at the beginning: significantly, it provided the catalyst for further investigations into the origins of jazz music.

While it is indisputable that many gifted players who have contributed greatly to the idiom are from parts distant from the Crescent City, the overwhelming weight of evidence from interviews, the written word and the gramophone

Above: Stalebread Lacoume's Spasm Band, 1899. Emile 'Stalebread' Lacoume, who went blind, is second from the left. His band was the only group mentioned in a famous book written about New Orleans in 1936, *The French Quarter* (right), by Herbert Asbury. His book gives the personnel of the band as follows: 'Willie Bussey, better known as Cajun, harmonica; Charley Stein, who manipulated an old kettle, a cowbell, a gourd filled with pebbles, and other traps [sic] and in later life became a famous drummer; Chinee, who smoked the bull fiddle, at first, half a barrel and later a coffin-shaped contraption built by the boys; Warm Gravy; Emile Benrod, called Whisky, and Frank Bussey, known as Monk.' *The French Quarter* is described on its jacket as: 'A gay account of the most sinful section of New Orleans when it was considered "The Wickedest City in the World".' Apart from mentioning the Spasm Band, Asbury fails to include reference to any other New Orleans jazz musicians, even omitting its most famous son, Louis Armstrong.

record is that this cosmopolitan city situated on the banks of the Mississippi produced an extraordinary number of unique musicians, whose collective activity truly fashioned jazz. One of its sons, trumpeter Louis Armstrong, became a household name throughout the world, a host of others were revered internationally, and many toured around the globe.

Settled by the French in about 1717, and named after the Duke of Orleans, then Regent in France, New Orleans was soon deserted. A second settlement in 1722 made more progress and New Orleans became the seat of government of the French territory of Louisiana. It continued to flourish after its cession to Spain in 1763. In 1800 it fell to France, from whom it was purchased in 1803 by the United States, together with the remainder of Louisiana. Ten years later it was incorporated into the United States,

Top left: Louis Armstrong's birthplace, c.1900. New Orleans was a city divided by class, as well as race, with a large section of the black population living in poverty.

Left: Armstrong (arrowed) spent a large part of his childhood in the coloured waif's home, where he at least had access to musical instruments.

Above: The bandstand at Tom Anderson's, Rampart Street, 1919, one of the most famous of the sporting houses, which employed a band. Illustrated here are Paul Barbarin, drums; Arnold Metoyer, trumpet; Luis Russell, piano; Willie Santiago, banjo; Albert Nicholas, clarinet and saxophones. Russell later had a band of his own 'fronted' by Louis Armstrong in the 1930s.

Right: The *New Orleans Blue Book* was supposed to have been financed by Tom Anderson. It offered entries such as 'Diana and Norma, 213–215 North Basin. Their names have become known on both continents, because everything goes as it will, and those that cannot be satisfied there must surely be of a queer nature.'

Blue Book

THIS BOOK MUST NOT BE MAILED

TO KNOW the right from the wrong, to be sure of yourself, go through this little book and read it carefully, and then when you visit Storyville you will know the best places to spend your money and time, as all the BEST houses are advertised. Read all the "ads."

This book contains nothing but Facts, and is of the greatest value to strangers when in this part of the city. The names of the residents will be found in this Directory, alphabetically arranged, under the headings "White" and "Colored," from alpha to omega. The names in capitals are landladies only.

You will find the boundary of the Tenderloin District, or Storyville: North side Iberville Street to south side St. Louis, and east side North Basin to west side North Robertson Street.

This is the boundary in which the women are compelled to live, according to law.

Above: The Superior Orchestra, 1910. Standing: Buddy Johnson, Bunk Johnson, 'Big Eye' Louis Nelson, Billy Marrero. Seated: Walter Brundy, Peter Bocage, Richard Payne. The Superior Orchestra was another marching band. Unexpected fame was to come Bunk Johnson's way 30 years later when there was a tremendous renaissance of interest in the old New Orleans musicians during what became known as 'the Revival'. Another band member who was later revered by the revivalists was 'Big Eye' Louis Nelson (pictured, **left**, many years later), a clarinettist of great power.

having become a port of entry the previous year. It was the capital of Louisiana until 1849, when it was superseded by Baton Rouge; fifteen years later it again became the seat of government, until it once more gave place to Baton Rouge in 1880. The population at the end of the 19th century was around 387,000. These bare historical facts, and the picture of slavery in the South, are the background of a multi-racial society with all the social conflicts and intermingling of cultures typical of such an environment, all of which had an enormous effect on

the musical development.

The generally warm climate throughout the year was a factor in the massive amount of open-air entertainment in which bands were employed. Among the characteristic institutions of New Orleans – probably stemming from successive military governments – were the marching bands, and from their ranks musicians emerged who were later to fashion the idiom that was to be called jazz. Without doubt the street bands were the breeding grounds for the jazz orchestras.

From its beginning New Orleans was

Above: Louis Armstrong, seen here with his mother Mayann and sister Beatrice, c.1918.

Top right: Kid Rena was born in New Orleans on 30th August 1898, and became a very powerful horn player. He met Louis Armstrong at the coloured waifs' home, where they were both tutored by Peter Davis. Rena died in New Orleans on 25th April 1949.

Above right: Freddie Keppard, born in New Orleans on 15th February 1889, was regarded as one of the top trumpet men in the city. He refused an invitation from the

Victor Label to make a recording in 1916, fearing that his ideas would be stolen by other musicians, and thus the honour of making the first jazz gramophone record fell to a white group – the Original Dixieland Jazz Band – a year later. Keppard died in Chicago on 15th July 1933.

known as the pleasure capital of the South, and acquired a notorious reputation for crime, corruption, gambling and, above all, prostitution, which thrived on the regular influx of visitors and the fact that it was a major seaport city. The element of prostitution which has fascinated historians of the city contributed to the development of jazz. The sporting houses generally did not employ 'formal' bands – a more appropriate music was called for which was not so loud as to disturb the other proceedings. This gave rise to a *genre* of piano players called 'professors', of which the redoubtable Ferdinand 'Jelly Roll' Morton was a very early member.

Bolden, too, was alleged to have played the 'houses'. One of the legends is that he exhorted his musicians to play:

'Way down, way down low
So I can hear them whores
Drag their feet across the floor'

An added exhortation was to females in the audience:

'Oh, you bitches,
shake your asses.'

NEVER CLOSED

TOM ANDERSON'S
Annex

COR. BASIN & IBERVILLE STS.

NOTED THE STATES
OVER *for* BEING THE
BEST CONDUCTED
CAFE *in* AMERICA

PRIVATE ROOMS *for the* FAIR SEX

MUSIC NIGHTLY
PHONES: 2253-Y & 2993-W
BILLY STRUVE *Manager*

Above: A prostitute in her 'crib'. Although many of the houses, such as this, were lavishly appointed, others, hardly more than squalid shacks, were obviously geared towards the lower end of the market.

Left: A poster advertising Tom Anderson's Annex and a detail from a scandal sheet called *The Sunday Sun*, which described Anderson's main establishment as follows: 'The Arlington Saloon, No. 12 N Rampart Street, presided over by Tom Anderson, is the principal and most popular resort for all sporting men. Everything you get there is first-class.'

Right: An early photograph of Ferdinand 'Jelly Roll' Morton, the most famous of the 'Piano Professors' in the Storyville sporting houses. Morton went on to become one of the foremost figures in jazz history.

THE ORIGINAL
CREOLE ORCHESTRA
1912

Above: The Original Creole Orchestra, c.1914. Standing: Eddie Vinson, trombone; Freddie Keppard, trumpet; George Baquet, clarinet; and Bill Johnson, bass. Seated: Dink Johnson, piano; James Palao, violin; and Norwood Williams, guitar. This was the first New Orleans band to 'go North' – to Chicago – but they regrettably made no records, and it is impossible to assess how much of a jazz unit they actually were.

Left: The Riverboat *Okahumkee*, c.1890. This was not one of the grander boats, but, as can be seen, it carried at least one musician (whether an employee or a passenger will never be known).

Many blacks and quite a few whites lived in abject poverty and frequented drinking places that were known as 'barrel houses', giving rise to the musical term applied to the piano players employed in these establishments. The red light district, although providing employment for musicians, mostly pianists, was only a segment of the entire New Orleans musical scene. Nevertheless its closure seriously restricted the employment opportunities.

In 1917 Storyville was closed down by the order of Secretary of the Navy Daniels, as venereal disease was rife among naval personnel. Mayor Martin Behrman complained bitterly, pronouncing that 'Pretermitting pros and cons of legislative recognition of prostitution as a necessary evil in a seaport the size of New Orleans, our city government has believed that the

Top: Buddy Petit's Jazz Band, Mandeville, Louisiana, 1920. Standing: Rene (second name unknown), megaphone; Eddie 'Face-O' Woods, drums; George Washington, trombone; Petit, trumpet; Edmond Hall, clarinet; Chester Zardis, bass. Seated is Bunny Manaday. The rural location is an interesting setting for what was, apparently, a rehearsal. Thirty-five years later Edmond Hall became a member of Louis Armstrong's All-Stars, and achieved international fame among enthusiasts.

Above: Jazz spread to New York and Chicago primarily by rail, but the riverboats helped to send the music out across the rest of the United States. The vessel illustrated here, the Streckfus liner *J.S.*, was obviously a much grander affair than the Okahumkee, and would have provided a full range of entertainments for its customers, including music and dancing. At various times it employed the bands of Fate Marable and Charlie Creath as 'resident' orchestras.

situation could be administered more easily and satisfactorily by confining it in a prescribed area. Our experience has taught us that the reasons for this are unanswerable, but the navy department of the Federal Government has decided otherwise.'

There have been various reports on the death of the red light district, some referring to pitiful scenes in the more famous – or infamous – of the streets: Basin, Franklin, Arberville, Bienville and St Louis. Here the byways were crammed with prostitutes wheeling out their possessions on carts and wheelbarrows to the strains of 'Nearer My God To Thee' played by a massive combination of black jazzmen. By that night the district was a ghost – rows upon rows of empty cribs. By this time there had been a considerable emigration from the South to the North by all sections of the coloured population, and the closing of Storyville was one more important factor in the exodus of the musicians.

Considering the history of the city, with its pleasure associations and its mixture of races, and the influence of the blues by the black population, it is no surprise that New Orleans produced the explosively

rumbustious and non-conformist music which was to spread throughout the world.

This chapter includes references to many early bands, largely black. While it is unfortunate that they were not recorded on gramophone records, it was marvellous that early photographers captured images of these pioneers for the benefit of posterity. Those reproduced in this section, many taken from that lovingly assembled and patently evocative compilation called *New Orleans Jazz – A Family Album* by Al Rose and Edmond Souchon, are a fascinating insight into the instrumentation, dress, demeanour and deportment of those early players. We are the privileged legatees of these photographs, which prompt us to wonder what sort of men the musicians were, and what kind of music they played, and to ponder on what connection exists between their endeavours and the sounds issuing from records and cassettes today.

It is appropriate that the first jazz band to make gramophone records was the Original Dixieland Jazz Band from New Orleans, in New York, early in 1917: this occasion was to start a train of events, the outstanding features of which this volume endeavours to embrace.

Above: The Fate Marable Band, c.1918. Baby Dodds, drums; Bill Ridgeley, trombone; Joe Howard, trumpet; unknown trumpeter; Marable at the piano; Dave Jones, mellophone; Johnny Dodds, clarinet; Johnny St Cyr, banjo; and Pops Foster, bass. They are seen here in the ballroom of one of the Mississippi riverboats which provided them with regular employment.

Right, top: John Stein's Original Dixieland Jazz Band, Chicago, 1916. Yellow Nunez, clarinet; Daddy Edwards, trombone; Henry Ragas, piano; Nick La Rocca, trumpet; Johnny Stein, drums. This was the nucleus of what became the Original Dixieland Jazz Band, under which title it became world famous and made the first ever jazz record.

Right: The Reliance Brass Band, 1910. Seated is leader Jack 'Papa' Laine. The rest of the line-up is: Manuel Mello, trumpet; Yellow Nunez, clarinet; Leonce Mello, trombone; Baby Laine, French horn; Chink Martin, euphonium; and Tim Harris, drums. Nunez later joined Stein's Original Dixieland Jazz Band line-up, with whom he is photographed (top), but had left them before they made their famous first recording.

The First Recordings

Enthusiasts and historians are still contesting the musical validity of those five young white men from New Orleans calling themselves the Original Dixieland Jazz Band who claimed to be the 'Creators of Jazz'.

The general consensus of opinion is that they were very limited in their inspiration and creativity, and that their phrasing was jerky, and their patterns were constantly repeated; but, as the English trumpeter and author Humphrey Lyttelton put it, in *The Best of Jazz*: 'They provided a sort of blueprint of how the line-up of trumpet, clarinet and trombone could be organized, and from tht blueprint came a lot more creative jazz in what has been called the Dixieland style.' Those Original Dixieland Jazz Band recording sessions were indeed to be the precursors of a flood of recordings by infinitely superior musicians from the Crescent City and elsewhere.

Left: A sheet music advertisement placed by the Melrose Brothers Music Company in the March 1924 issue of *Metronome*.

Below: A contemporary cartoon of the Original Dixieland Jazz Band. The frenetic activity illustrated fully reflects the promotional literature issued by the band's record label – Victor – at the time: '. . . only with the greatest of effort were we able to make the Original Dixieland Jazz Band sit still long enough to make a record.'

The Original Dixieland Jazz Band and its Imitators

Left: The Original Dixieland Jazz Band, 1917. Tony Sbarbaro, drums (though seen here with a trumpet to his lips); Eddie Edwards, trombone; Nick La Rocca, trumpet; Larry Shields, clarinet, and Henry Ragas, piano. This was not the first 'Original' Dixieland Jazz Band, but it was the one that made the initial historic recordings, the first jazz ever on shellac. They recorded while making a sensational appearance at the 400 Room, and claimed, as this picture shows, to be the 'Creators of Jazz'.

Below: Bailey's Lucky Seven (The Original Memphis Five) in the Gennett studios. Note the distance between the trumpeter and the recording horn.

Right: Kid Ory's Creole Jazz Band, Los Angeles, 1921/2.

Other 'Original' Jazz Bands

Understandably, the success of the Original Dixieland Jazz Band encouraged bands with a similar instrumentation and style to make gramophone records, and some carried through their imitation as far as including the word 'Original' in their title – such as the Original New Orleans Band and The Original Memphis Five. Three bands at least – The Original New Orleans Band, The Louisiana Five, and the Whiteway Jazz Band – had as much right to be on shellac as the Original Dixieland Jazz Band because of the New Orleans musicians in their personnel. The Louisiana Five, for example, included Yellow Nunez, who was Larry Shields' immediate predecessor in the Original Dixieland Jazz Band. The most successful and long-lasting

of these rivals was the Original Memphis Five, albeit that not one of them was from Memphis, or, indeed, anywhere in the South. Its most outstanding musician was Miff Mole. Their first recording, made in New York in April 1922, was shamelessly released by the record company under the name of the Original Dixieland Jazz Band.

Kid Ory's Original Creole Jazz Band was the first black New Orleans band to make gramophone records (other black musicians had recorded previously, but the results are of limited jazz value), and was sometimes billed as Kid Ory's Brown-Skinned Babies. The line-up is: Baby Dodds, drums; Ory, trombone; Mutt Carey, trumpet; Ed Garland at the piano, with his instrument, the bass, in the

foreground; and Wade Whaley, clarinet. The band that recorded for the Sunshine label in Los Angeles in June 1922 comprised Carey, Ory, and Garland, with Dink Johnson, clarinet; Fred Washington, piano; and Ben Borders on drums. The two titles were 'Ory's Creole Trombone' (which he was to re-record many times over, with Armstrong, among others) and 'Society Blues', and the record was released under the name of Spikes' Seven Pods of Pepper, as the label was run by the Spikes Brothers. Only a few copies were released, and an original is now a great rarity, though the recording has been included in many compilations.

Initially the Dixielanders were billed as a 'jass' band, a title that also appeared on their first record labels. (The story goes that children, of all ages, removed the 'j' from the posters.) Their first recordings, 'Darktown Strutters Ball' and 'Indiana' were made for the Columbia label on 30th January 1917, but the company executives were so horrified by the 'cacophony' that they immediately shelved the masters. Barely a month later the band recorded for the Victor label, also in New York, 'Livery Stable Blues' and 'Dixie Jass Band One-Step'. The world's first jazz record was boldly launched with a special issue of the *Victor Record Review*, dated 17th March 1917. The blurb, after first warning the customer that 'A jass band is a jass band and not a Victor Organization gone crazy', introduced the new sound in the following vein:

'Spell it Jass, Jas, Jaz or Jazz – nothing can spoil a jazz band. Some say the jazz band originated in Chicago. Chicago says it comes from San Francisco – San Francisco being away off

Below: The New Orleans Owls, 1924. Dick Mackie, cornet; Monk Smith, saxophone; Red Mackie, piano; Benji White, saxophone; Eblen Rau, bass; René Gelpi, banjo; and Earl Crumb, drums. This was one of the few bands to be recorded in New Orleans during the 1920s, although not always with the original personnel shown here.

Right: A feature article on the origins of the word 'jazz', written by Ernest J. Hopkins, appeared in the *San Francisco Bulletin* in 1913, adding further to a debate that has never been fully resolved. The article is reproduced here from the December 1973 issue of *Storyville* (No. 50).

Below right: Sam Morgan's Jazz Band. This band went virtually unnoticed, with their recordings probably only selling in the New Orleans area. Decades later they reappeared on various compilations. Jim Robinson went on to become a member of the Bunk Johnson and George Lewis bands.

In Praise of "Jazz," a Futurist Word Which Has Just Joined the Language.

THIS COLUMN is entitled "What's not in the news," but occasionally a few things that are in the news leak in. We have been trying for some time to keep one of those things out, but hereby acknowledge ourselves powerless and surrender.

THIS THING IS a word. It has recently become current in The Bulletin office, through some means which we cannot discover but would stop up if we could. There should be every precaution taken to avoid the possibility of any more such words leaking in to disturb our vocabularies.

THIS WORD IS "JAZ." It is also spelt "Jazz," and as they both sound the same and mean the same, there seems to be no way of settling the controversy. The office staff is divided into two sharp factions, one of which upholds the single z and the other the double z. To keep them from coming to blows, much Christianity is required.

"JAZZ" (WE CHANGE the spelling each time so as not to offend either faction) can be defined, but it cannot be synonymized. If there were another word that exactly expressed the meaning of "jaz," "Jazz" would never have been born. A new word, like a new muscle, only comes into being when it has been long needed.

This remarkable and satisfactory-sounding word, however, means something like life, vigor, energy, effervescence of spirit, joy, pep, magnetism, verve, virility, ebulliency, courage, happiness—oh, what's the use?—JAZZ. Nothing else can express it.

WHEN YOU SMILE at the office-boy (time, 7:30 a.m.) as though you thought him nice, that is "jaz." When you hit the waiter for serving you cold waffles, that is "jaz." When you work until midnight, then get up and work until midnight again without cursing your boss, that is "jaz." When you look upon a girl and she loves you, that is "jaz."

Some idea of the utter usefulness and power of this wonderful word now begins to appear.

YOU CAN GO ON flinging the new word all over the world, like a boy with a new jack-knife. It is "jazz" when you run for your train; "jaz" when you soak the umpire; "jazz" when you demand a raise; "jaz" when you hike thirty-five miles of a Sunday; "jazz" when you simply sit around and beam so that all who look beam on you. Anything that takes manliness or effort or energy or activity or strength of soul is "jaz."

WE WOULD NOT have you apprehend that this new word is slang. It is merely futurist language, which as everybody knows is more than mere cartooning.

"Jazz" is a nice word, a classic word, easy on the tongue and pleasant to the ears, profoundly expressive of the idea it conveys—as when you say a home-run hitter is "full of the old jaz." (Credit Scoop.) There is, and always has been, an art of genial strength; to this art we now victoriously give the splendid title of "Jazz."

THE SHEER MUSICAL quality of the word, that delightful sound like the crackling of a brisk electric spark, commends it. It belongs to the class of onomatopoeia. It was important that this vacancy in our language should have been filled with a word of proper sound, because "jaz" is a quality often celebrated in epic poetry in prizefight stories, in the tale of action or the meditative sonnet. It is a universal word, and must appear well in all society.

That is why "pep," which tried to mean the same but never could, failed. It was a rough-neck from the first, and could not wear evening clothes. "Jaz" is at home in bar or ballroom; it is a true American.

TO CONCLUDE, JUST a few examples of its use.

"Miss Eugenia Jefferson-Lord was clad in a pink pongee creation suitable for a rainy day, and of great jaz." (Society Notes.)

"Our Harry, sighting true for once, swung the willow against the pill with all his jazz." (Baseball account.)

"Though fatally shot, the unfortunate captain still had sufficient jaz to murmur 'He done it' in the ears of the police." (Murder story.)

"All the worl' am done gone crazy,
Yassah, sure it has,
How mah brain am reeling, dazy,
Sighin' for the ol', ol' jazz!"
(Plantation melody.)

"And Saturn strode athwart the cedarn grove,
Filled with the jaz that makes Creation move!" (Paradise Lost.)
—ERNEST J. HOPKINS.

again to me in person when we met — that Jazz was a nice word — though he was entirely prophetic in saying "Jazz" is at home in bar or ballroom — it is a true American.

Facts from the Great Authority

Up to this point — April, 1913 — everyone seems to have heard the word Jazz from someone else. Ray Lopez heard it from Bill Demarest who heard it from his brother. Bert Kelly heard it from Miguel Luna and Harry Warren. Scoop Gleeson heard it from Slattery. Ernest Hopkins heard it from Walter Harrison. And so on. It was a nice word. It was a naughty one. They tried to pin it on madams, immigrants, gamblers, slaves, poets. Nobody knew or cared where the word originally came from — or how to spell it — but it was, as Ernest Hopkins said, "New, long-needed, satisfactory-sounding, peppy, versatile ....like the crackling of a brisk electric spark."

The word really surfaced in late 1914 or 1915 in Chicago. I won't take time here to detail the particulars. It certainly achieved notoriety, if not fame, as a musical term. And before you knew it, the "jazz band" was full-blown and taking root. Yet surprisingly enough, no one delved into the etymology of the word. For example: William Ernest Henley and John Stephen Farmer published a seven-volume glossary of *Slang and Its Analogues* in editions published before 1910, but there is no mention of Jazz (any spelling). Henry Edward Krehbiel, a noted music critic and lecturer in the 1880s and 1890s, had a lengthy correspondence with Lafcadio Hearn regarding Creoles, Negroes, music and dances ....but never Jazz. Nor did he use the word in his *Afro-American Folksongs*, published in 1914. Our word Jazz is not in the 1906 monograph *La Musique Chez les Peuples Indigènes de l'Amerique du Nord*, published in Paris by Julien Tiersot, Librarian of the Paris Conservatory. The plain fact is that the word Jazz was not researched up to (and including!) August of 1917. That's when the great literary hoax was perpetrated by the plausible Eng and

across the continent. Anyway, a Jazz band is the newest thing in cabarets, greatly adding to the hilarity thereof . . . Since then the Jass band has grown in size and ferocity, and only with the greatest effort were we able to make the Original Dixieland Jass Band stand still long enough to make a record. That's the difficulty with a Jass band. You never know what it's going to do next, but you can always tell what those who hear it are going to do – they're going to 'shake a leg'.

The Jass Band is the very latest thing in the development of music. It has sufficient power and penetration to inject new life into a mummy, and will keep ordinary human dancers on their feet till breakfast time . . ?

Soon, Jass and other spellings like Jasz went by the board, and 'Jazz' was now included in the band's title and in the titles of their tunes. Thenceforward, this was the generally accepted spelling applied to all music of this kind.

The First Recordings

Left: King Oliver's Creole Jazz Band. Standing: King Oliver, trumpet; Bill Johnson, bass and banjo. Seated: Baby Dodds, drums; Honore Dutrey, trombone; Louis Armstrong, trumpet; Johnny Dodds, clarinet; and Lil Hardin, Armstrong's future wife, at the piano.

Below left: The New Orleans Rhythm Kings, 1922. Leon Roppolo, clarinet; Jack Pettis, C melody saxophone; Elmer Schoebel, piano; Arnold Loyacano, bass; Paul Mares, cornet; Frank Snyder, drums; and George Brunies, trombone.

Below: The Wolverine Orchestra. Standing: Dick Voynow, piano. Seated: Vic Moore, drums; George Johnson, saxophone; Jimmy Hartwell, clarinet; Bix Beiderbecke, trumpet; Al Gande, trombone; Min Leibrook, tuba; Bob Gillette, banjo.

Right: King Oliver (seated) and Louis Armstrong, 1922. A historic shot of the two New Orleans trumpet giants, who combined to make a remarkable series of recordings for the Gennett label.

Far right: An advertisement from Gennett, proudly featuring their list of coloured artists.

Recording Information of Wax No. 11854
11854A
11854B

Date Recorded 5-6-24   By E. C. A. Wickemeyer   At Richmond, Ind.

Subject Riverboat Shuffle

By Wolverine Orchestra   Accompanied by

Composed by   Music by Carmichael

Words by Carmichael   Published by Hoaglund Carmichael
Kappa Sigma House, Bloomington, Indiana

Copyright   19   Royalties   1924

AUdubon 3-0424

JELLY ROLL MORTON'S
ORCHESTRA
Originator of JAZZ - STOMP - SWING
VICTOR ARTIST
World's greatest Hot Tune Writer

209 West 131st Street   New York City

JELLY ROLL MORTON'S ORCHESTRA
209 West 131st Street   New York City
AUdubon 3-0424
Originator of JAZZ - STOMP - SWING
VICTOR ARTIST
World's Greatest Hot Tune Writer
Music Furnished For All Occasions
Nothing too Large, Nothing too small
15 Pieces or Less

The sales of their first Victor issue ran into hundreds of thousands without, as has been claimed, quite becoming a million-seller. Of course, it is possible these many decades later, considering the number of times this record has been re-released in album compilations, that it may well have sold near a million by now – an extraordinary feat for the first-ever jazz record released.

If the general public took to the novelty, the New Orleans *Times-Picayune* was not impressed by the success of their sons who had gone North. In its 20th June 1918 issue, the editorial carried the following condemnation:

'Why is the jass music, and therefore a jazz band? As well ask why is the dime novel, or the grease-dripping dough-nut? All are manifestations of a low streak in man's tastes that has not yet come out in civilization's wash. Indeed, one might go further and say that

Top: The information sheet for the recording of 'Riverboat Shuffle' by the Wolverline Orchestra at the Gennett Studios. 'Carmichael' refers to Hoagy Carmichael (**above**), the prolific composer whose songs included 'Stardust', and who was a close friend of Beiderbecke. The personnel for this recording is as depicted on the previous page, except for trombonist Al Gande, who had by this time left the band.

Above right, and right: Some 'Jelly Roll' Morton ephemera: his calling cards, and a notable record label with his name incorrectly spelt.

Far right: Throughout his career Ferdinand 'Jelly Roll' Morton was a colourful New Orleans figure, who started his activities in the 'district' well before the First World War,

not only playing the piano, but hustling in a variety of dubious enterprises, including pimping and playing pool to supplement his earnings. He led a nomadic existence, subsidized by his musical and non-musical endeavours, and finally commenced recording in 1921 for the Paramount label. These early records are of no great value, and cannot compare with the later Red Hot Peppers sessions made for the Victor label in 1926. He also recorded for the Vocalion label in the early 1920s.

PRICE 75c
TRADE MARK   REGISTERED
Paramount
12050-A   Instrumental
Blue
Big Fat Ham
Jelly Roll Marton and His
Orchestra
1434
THE NEW YORK RECORDING LABORATORIES, INC. • PORT WASHINGTON, WIS.

3261

Address:- c/o Melrose Music Co., 177 No.State St., Chicago, Ill.
Records by: JELLY-ROLL MORTON'S RED HOT PEPPERS (Colored)

3 — *continued*

Marking	Letter	Pitch	Serial No.	Matris No.	Selection, Composer, Publisher, Copyright, Etc. (FM-HG)	Wax.	Rec.	F. Cur.	Level	Amp. Set	Eqlsr.	Fil.
					Chicago——Webster Hotel-December,16th.1926. Instr:-2 Violins-Cornet-Trombone-Clarinet-Banjo-St.Bass Piano & Trapman.							
P	BVE	100	37254	1	Someday Sweetheart — Blues	55-135R	24	.7	H-4-5	16	On	20
M	BVE	100	37254	2	Comp. Spikes & Spikes (John & Benjamin)	55-158	"	"	H-3-4	4	"	16
H30	BVE	100	37254	3	Pub. & Copyr., Melrose Bros., Music Co.,1924.	55-158	"	"	H-6-4	8	"	14
P	BVE	96	37255	1	Grandpa's Spells — Stomp	55-145R	"	"	H-5-6	10	"	16
H30	BVE	96	37255	2	Comp. Jelly Roll Morton, (date is)	55-122	"	"	H-4-5	8	"	"
M	BVE	96	37255	3	Pub. & Copyr., Melrose Bros.,Music Co.(1925, verbal)	55-122	"	"	H-3-4	6	"	14
H30	BVE	96	37256	1	Original Jelly Roll Blues	55-158	"	"	H-5-4	10	"	16
M	BVE	96	37256	2	Comp. Jelly Roll Morton, Pub. & Copyr.,Melrose Bros.,1926 (Verbal by Mr.Melrose)	55-135R	"	"	H-5-3	8	"	14
P	BVE	100	37257	1	Doctor Jazz Stomp (Vocal by Jelly R.Morton)	55-150	"	"	H-4-3	16	"	16
H30	BVE	100	37257	2	Comp. Joe Oliver,	55-121R	"	"	H-4-3	8	"	14
M	BVE	100	37257	3	Pub. & Copyr.,Melrose Bros.,1926 (Verbal by Mr. Melrose)	55-150	"	"	H-5-3	8	"	"
H30	BVE	100	37258	1	Cannon Ball Blues	55-150	"	"	H-5-3	8	"	16
M	BVE	100	37258	2	Comp.Rider Bloom & Jelly R.Morton, Pub. & Copyr.,Melrose Bros.,1926 (Verbal by Mr. Melrose) Time 1:30 to 6:00 PM	55-158	"	"	H-4-3	6	"	14

Top: 'Jelly Roll' Morton's Red Hot Peppers, 1926. Andrew Hilaire, drums; Kid Ory, trombone; George Mitchell, trumpet; John Lindsay, bass; Morton, at the piano; Johnny St Cyr, banjo; and Omar Simeon, clarinet. Hilaire, Lindsay, St Cyr, Morton

and Simeon were from New Orleans; George Mitchell, from Louisville, Kentucky, was the 'outsider', but fitted Morton's requirements perfectly. Their recordings are regarded as classics, and are constantly reissued.

Above: The Victor recording card for one of the Red Hot Peppers 1926 sessions. Five titles with alternative 'takes', making a total of 13 recordings in one day. Note the reference to the performers' race, in brackets after the band's name.

Jass music is the indecent story syncopated and counterpointed. Like the improper anecdote, also, in its youth, it was listened to blushingly behind closed doors and drawn curtains, but, like all vice, it grew bolder until it dared decent surroundings, and there was tolerated because of its oddity . . .

In the matter of jass, New Orleans is particularly interested, since it has been widely suggested that this particular form of musical vice had its birth in this city, that it came, in fact, from doubtful surroundings in our slums. We do not recognize the honor of parenthood, but with such a story in circulation, it behooves us to be last to accept the atrocity in polite society, and where it has crept in we should make it a point of civic honor to suppress it. Its musical value is nil, and its possibilities of harm are great.'

A few days later, the *Times-Picayune* received and published an angry letter

TRafalgar 6-9320

CLARENCE WILLIAMS, Sr.
"The Originator of Jazz and "Boogie-Woogie"
Composer, Playright, Producer and Pianist
Radio, Recording and Motion Picture Artist

717A MADISON STREET   BROOKLYN 21, N. Y.

Top: Sydney Bechet, Clarence Williams, and Louis Armstrong, 1940. Clarence Williams, pianist, composer and bandleader, was one of the few coloured artists to run his own publishing business. He organized and played on hundreds of sessions and was responsible for Sydney Bechet's first recordings, with Clarence Williams' Blue Five in 1923. In 1924 the Blue Five personnel included Louis Armstrong in addition to Bechet. **Above** is some Williams ephemera; a business card on which he

claimed to be 'The Originator of Jazz and Boogie-Woogie', and a fine caricature by Dutch artist Boy ten Hove.

from a reader who resented the editorial remarks about his favourite delicacy – the grease-dripping dough-nut. Amid this furore the *Ladies Home Journal* of August 1921 showed concern by enquiring 'Does Jazz put the sin in syncopation?'

At the height of their fame, the Original Dixieland Jazz Band elected to accept an offer to play in England and in January 1919 they sailed on the *RMS Adriatic* for the United Kingdom, arriving at Liverpool on 1st April.

After the success of the Original Dixieland Jazz Band, Columbia (who, it will be recalled, had taken their recording of the band off their shelves) despatched their Artistes and Repertoire chief, Ralph Peers, to New Orleans with a brief to contract other bands from that city. After three weeks Peers wired back – 'No jazz bands in New Orleans' – and, returning home via Memphis, signed up WC Handy and his Orchestra who commenced recording for the company in New York in September 1917.

Handy was dubbed 'Father of the Blues' as many blues compositions bore his name, including the most famous of

GENERAL PHONOGRAPH CORPORATION

Record Laboratory

9484-a

DATE ....Nov 12, 1925
Recorded by ....D

Laboratory No. .... Size 10"
Catalogue No. 8320-B
Coupled with 9535 a
Special Catalogue No. June 5, 1926

Selection ....Dry Heart
By Louis Armstrong and His Hot Five ....Accompanied by ....
Composed by ....Lillian Armstrong
From ....
Publisher ....Consolidated Music Pub. House ....Copyright ....76.... 19
Address ....227 W. Washington St., Chicago, Ill
I sent contract 5-24-26

Remarks ....Race
Made in Chicago Ill ....2 cent
white — 2. 50

Far left, above: Advertisement for the 'St James Infirmary Blues'.

Far left, below and left: Record labels of recordings by the Hot Five, and a recording by Bertha 'Chippie' Hill on which Armstrong was an accompanist.

Above: OKEH information sheet for a recording of 'Dry Heart', by Armstrong's Hot Five, made on 12th November 1925.

Left: Louis Armstrong's Hot Five, 1926. Johnny St Cyr, banjo; Kid Ory, trombone; Louis Armstrong, trumpet; Johnny Dodds, clarinet; and Lil Armstrong, piano. The Hot Five and Hot Seven were confined almost wholly to the recording studio, and their sessions are now regarded as masterpieces. Armstrong continued recording with his Hot Five and Hot Seven until 1928, producing virtually the last examples of small group improvization in the classic style before the big bands were in complete ascendancy. It was not until the mid-1940s that Armstrong reverted to the small group format and became an integral part of the 'Revival'.

all, 'St Louis Blues', but history has designated him as more a collector and notator of the blues in general currency, and his band was patently no jazz band. In 1921, trumpeter Johnny Dunn and his Jazz Hounds made their first recordings and Dunn accompanied blues singer Mamie Smith on what was the first best-selling blues record, 'Crazy Blues', but these and other recordings by Eastern musicians (usually accompanying singers) had variable jazz content.

The honour of being the first black jazz band proper fell to Kid Ory's Creole Jazz Band in Los Angeles in 1922, which comprised of New Orleans musicians. Their claim to be the first genuine jazz band to record stands up. It is perhaps surprising, considering that the Original Dixieland Jazz Band made their first

record back in 1917, that it should be five years later before a bona fide black jazz band was committed to wax. It was as if recording executives shied clear of black bands, perhaps thinking that the playing was not 'clean' enough for white consumption.

The fact that the first recordings of a black New Orleans band should have been made on home equipment in a publisher's back room is one of the piquant facts of early jazz history. Another is that other famous early recordings, the most significant of which were by King Oliver's Creole Jazz Band, were made in a ramshackle building in Richmond, Indiana. The Oliver recordings, made for the Gennett label, featured the 23-year-old Louis Armstrong on second cornet behind King Oliver's lead. They made

Below: A Gennett label for a recording of 'That Sweet Something Dear' by King Oliver and his Creole Jazz Band.

Above: The New Orleans Rhythm Kings, c.1922. George Brunies, trombone; Paul Mares, trumpet; Ben Pollack, drums; Leon Roppolo, saxophone; Mel Stitzel, piano; Volly De Faut, clarinet and saxophone; Lew Black, banjo; and Steve Brown, bass and sousaphone.

Above right: Gennett studios. The Gennett Record Company and label was owned by the Starr piano Company of Richmond, Indiana. Their recording equipment was primitive and frequently broke down; the room was poorly ventilated, and all activity had to cease while the trains rumbled by. Nevertheless, the label is fondly regarded by enthusiasts for the many classic recordings made there.

Right: Red Nichols (left) and Miff Mole were the personifications of 'white' jazz. Although the instrumentation they used on hundreds of recordings was similar to that employed by Louis Armstrong and 'Jelly Roll' Morton, their phrasing and tonal values were very different. They recorded under several titles, including the Red and Miff Stompers; Red Nichols and his Five Pennies; the Red Heads; Miff Mole and the Molers, and the Charleston Chasers.

nine sides, all recorded on one day – 16th April 1923. These were recorded at the Gennett Studio, a catacomb of wood-panelled rooms in a decrepit framed warehouse set alongside a weed-grown section of railway siding in the middle of the industrial section of the town. The primitive acoustic equipment did little justice to their free-wheeling collective improvization, but the sheer force of the ensemble drive generated via Oliver and Armstrong on trumpets, with Johnny Dodds on clarinet interweaving, led to the recordings being regarded as classics in later years.

Other recordings on the Gennett label were made by the New Orleans Rhythm Kings, a white band playing principally in their home town; a band from the East, the Wolverines, led by the legendary Bix Beiderbecke; and Beiderbecke and His Rhythm Jugglers, a band that included a young trombonist later to become world-famous, Tommy Dorsey.

Despite the increasing move towards bigger bands the 1920s was a fecund period of small-band endeavours, producing hundreds upon hundreds of recordings that to this day appear on numerous compilations.

Top left: Mezz Mezzrow (far left) and Frank Teschemacher (far right) hold an important place as founding members of the Chicago school – a whole new phase of jazz.

Far left: A young Jean Goldkette, c.1927. In the years before he became a band contractor, he was a classical pianist.

Left: Paul Mertz, pianist and member of Bix and his Rhythm Jugglers, who also went on to join Goldkette.

Above: Bix and his Rhythm Jugglers in Gennett Studios, 26th January 1925. Don Murray, clarinet; Howdy Quicksell, banjo; Tom Gargano, drums; Paul Mertz, piano; Beiderbecke, cornet; and Tommy Dorsey, trombone. This was the first band to work under Beiderbecke's name.

Right: The Austin High School Gang, a group of young white Chicagoans, including Teschemacher, who fell under the spell of the numerous black musicians playing in the area and decided to become jazzmen themselves.

The Birth of the Big Bands

With one or two exceptions the Armstrong Hot Five's and Hot Seven's were the last of the small black bands recording in the 1920s. The trend from then on was towards larger orchestras, a pattern originally set by Paul Whiteman, one of the first band leaders to 'refine' jazz by introducing harmonized arrangements, and by virtually doing away with solo improvization. In 1920 he had a million-seller record, 'Wang Wang Blues' (which wasn't a blues), and followed this in the same year with 'Whispering', backed by 'Japanese Sandman'. Whiteman became known as the King of Jazz.

The first black orchestra of distinction was led by a former chemistry student from Cuthbert, Georgia, pianist/arranger Fletcher 'Smack' Henderson. He entered the music industry in 1921 as a recording manager for Black Swan Records, working mainly with black artistes, and went on to provide the accompaniments to a succession of blues singers. At first his band was extremely stiff – hardly

Top left: Fletcher Henderson and his Club Alabam Orchestra, 1924. An unknown trombonist (possibly Teddy Nixon); Howard Scott and Elmer Chambers, trumpets; Ralph Escudero, tuba; Fletcher Henderson, piano (seated); Clarence Robinson, dancer; Charlie Dixon, banjo; Kaiser Marshall, drums; and Coleman Hawkins and Don Redman, reeds. The extent of Redman's multi-instrumental virtuosity is indicated by the rack he required to accommodate his array of instruments.

Left: An advertisement in the Baltimore *Afro American*, 27th July 1929.

Above: Bigger bands needed bigger locations. The famous *Roseland Ballroom*, seen here in a photograph from the 1920s, was a favourite location of Henderson's orchestra and many other black bands, and incorporated a double bandstand. Situated at that time on the corner of Broadway and 51st, it later moved to 52nd Street, where it doubled in size.

Right: A publicity photograph of Fletcher Henderson from the late 1920s.

distinguishable from all the white bands that followed in the wake of Whiteman – but with the enlistment of tenor saxophonist Coleman Hawkins, clarinettist Buster Bailey, trombonist Charlie Green, and, for a brief period, Louis Armstrong, it developed into a major force. It was the precursor of 'swing' and, ironically, he was to be an arranger for the King of Swing – Benny Goodman – in the 1930s,

while his own band, with a much greater array of soloists, was struggling.

Next came Duke Ellington, whose first band comprised only five pieces, but was to be the beginning of the greatest jazz orchestra ever. His talents as a composer and arranger, and his ability to enlist outstanding soloists, combined to form the basis of the Ellington sound. Along with a handful of other black jazzmen – Louis

Armstrong, Dizzy Gillespie and Miles Davis – Ellington is among the most famous of all the jazz giants, and his name is known throughout the world both inside and outside jazz circles.

By 1926 King Oliver had forsaken the classic line-up to go along with the fashion of larger instrumentation, and his new band was to include other New Orleanians, trombonist Kid Ory, clarinettists Barney

Right: An advertisement for King Oliver and his Dixieland Syncopators, placed by their label, Vocalion Records. King Oliver departed from the classic New Orleans ensemble with which he recorded for Gennett, OKEH and Columbia in the mid-1920s to form this medium-sized band. It relied heavily on arrangements rather than collective improvization, but included a high incidence of New Orleans musicians to give it the stamp of quality.

Below right: An information sheet from 1926 detailing a recording session by Duke Ellington and his Washingtonians.

Below: An early publicity photograph of Duke Ellington. Ellington was born in Washington DC, 29th April 1899.

Above: King Oliver's Dixieland Syncopators, c.1926. Standing: Bert Cobb, tuba; Paul Barbarin, drums; King Oliver and Bob Shoffner, trumpets. Seated: George Field, trombone; Bud Scott, banjo; Darnell Howard, Albert Nicholas and Barney Bigard, reeds; and Luis Russell, piano.

Left: Duke Ellington's Washingtonians at the Kentucky Club, 1923. Standing: Sonny Greer, drums; Charlie Irvis, trombone; Elmer Snowden, banjo; Otto Hardwicke, alto saxophone. Seated: Bubber Miley, trumpet; and Duke Ellington, piano. This was one of the Duke's early bands, and its recordings gave little evidence of the extraordinary creativity which evolved in later manifestations. Ellington gradually increased his personnel until it eventually became the most formidable combination in the history of the idiom.

Henderson Record Labels

During his career, Henderson material was released by a huge range of labels, owned by various companies. As well as those seen here – Diva, Columbia, Puritan, Black Swan, Melody, Oriole, Olympic, and Brunswick (re-released on UHCA/ Commodore) – labels under which his work was issued included Allegro, Star Dust, Vocalion, Victor, Apex, Ajax, Regal, Music Service, National, Perfect, and Paramount.

AND HIS 'OLD MAN RIVER' ORCHESTRA

Bigard, and Albert Nicholas. Although his big band recordings are collectors' items, the venture was not a commercial success, and he missed the opportunity of a lifetime by turning down an offer to be the resident band at the Cotton Club – the engagement that later launched Duke Ellington to international fame. In 1928 the core of the band was taken over by Luis Russell, and thereafter Oliver's fortunes declined, although he continued to lead bands into the mid-1930s. Reduced to poverty, his last days were spent as a pool-room attendant. Had he survived a few more years he would at least have benefited from the royalties on the tunes he composed, which came to be played the world over during the 'Revival'.

Above: Luis Russell's Old Man River Orchestra. Russell was a Storyville pianist who took over King Oliver's Dixie Syncopators in the late 1920s, and went on to fashion a band regarded as one of the hottest ever. Its scintillating line-up of soloists included at various times: trumpeters Red Allen, Bill Coleman, and Rex Stewart; trombonists JC Higginbotham and Dickie Wells; alto saxophonist Charlie Holmes; clarinettist Albert Nicholas; and a pounding rhythm section comprising of Russell, Paul Barbarin, Pops Foster, and Will Johnson.

The First of the Big Bands

Left: Luis Russell magnificently caricatured by Boy ten Hove. Russell was born in Panama on August 6th 1902, and died in New York on 11th December 1963.

Below: Benny Pollack's Orchestra, 1927. Larry Binyon, tenor saxophone; Benny Goodman, clarinet; Gil Rodin, alto saxophone; Al Lasker, tuba; Pollack, drums; Al Gifford, banjo; Wayne Allen, piano (and arranger); Al Harris and Harry Greenberg, trumpets; and Glenn Miller, trombone. Benny Pollack was born in Toluca Illinois on 22nd December 1901. He began his career with the New Orleans Rhythm Kings, and in 1926 founded the first of several jazz-oriented dance bands. He is remembered for the considerable amount of solo space he gave to his young bloods. He died in Chicago on 11th July 1949.

Once Luis Russell became leader he brought in the New Orleans trumpeter Red Allen and the Georgia-born trombonist JC Higginbotham; they made some outstanding recordings before the band was taken over in turn by Louis Armstrong in 1935, when it assumed a supporting role to the 'act' of the trumpeter/singer. Russell's career, like Oliver's, suffered a decline. During the early 1960s he was working as a chauffeur. Before taking over the Russell band, Armstrong had appeared with and led a variety of bands ranging from seven to ten pieces, but which always principally functioned as a background for the leader's soaring solo flights.

In the white bands there was predominately a heavy emphasis on harmonized arrangements with very few solos. One exception was the band led by drummer Benny Pollack which made a special feature of its star soloists, including clarinettist Benny Goodman, trombonist Jack Teagarden, and, later, trumpeters Harry James and Muggsy Spanier. Probably because he allowed his soloists their heads, Pollack enjoyed only relative commercial

Above: Jean Goldkette and his Orchestra, 1926/7. Goldkette's organization controlled over 20 bands, although he didn't actually play in any of them. His 1926/7 band contained a cadre of young jazzmen who gave the band its real character. Among the finest of them were Frank (sometimes 'Frankie') Trumbauer, saxophone (third from the left in the highest group, with a colleague's hand on his shoulder), and Bix Beiderbecke, trumpet (seen contentedly lounging on the bonnet, his head level with the roof of the bus). Both achieved individual fame, though sadly Beiderbecke died only a few years later, in 1931.

Right: Detail from an EMI album cover – 'Bix & Tram – 1927' – showing Beiderbecke (left) and Trumbauer.

CLARINET MARMALADE
SINGIN' THE BLUES
OSTRICH WALK
RIVERBOAT SHUFFLE
I'M COMING VIRGINIA
'WAY DOWN YONDER IN NEW ORLEANS
THREE BLIND MICE
BLUE RIVER
THERE'S A CRADLE IN CAROLINE
HUMPTY DUMPTY
KRAZY KAT
BALTIMORE
JUST AN HOUR OF LOVE
I'M WONDERIN' WHO
CRYING ALL DAY
A GOOD MAN IS HARD TO FIND

Early Black Big Bands

Left: Speed Webb and his Hollywood Blue Devils, 1929. This was a 'territory' band, a term for orchestras operating outside the big cities of New York, Chicago, and Kansas City. His was one of the first bands to work in the Hollywood studios, a fact he capitalized upon in his publicity material.

Right: Louis Armstrong's first big band, 1929. Throughout the 1920s, Armstrong played with various big orchestras, while still recording with small groups. 1929 saw him completely abandon the small group format, to which he did not return until the 1940s.

Below: Bennie Moten and his Orchestra, 1930. This band was the biggest name in Kansas City jazz in the 1920s, having started out as a small group based on the instrumentation and style of King Oliver's Creole Jazz Band. Its stars included trumpeters Ed Lewis, Paul Webster, and Oran 'Hot Lips' Page; saxophonists Jack Washington, Harlan Leonard, and Ben Webster; vocalist Jimmy Rushing; and pianist Count Basie.

Above right: Zack Whyte and his Chocolate Beau Brummels, 1929. This was a lesser known but very active coloured black band of the 1920s, which at times included trumpeter Roy Eldridge; trombonists Vic Dickenson and Quentin Jackson; pianist Herman Chittison; and tenor saxophonist Al Sears. The band survived the hazards of recording for the Gennett label, which issued several of their recordings, including (**top left**) 'Mandy'.

Above: An early publicity photograph of William McKinney.

Right: A poster advertizing McKinney's Cotton Pickers in properly glowing terms. One of the greatest bands of the era, it operated mainly in the Detroit area, and included in its personnel: Dave Wilborn, banjo and guitar; Prince Robinson, Don Redman, George Thomas, and Milton Senior, reeds; John Nesbit and Langston Curl, trumpets; Claude Jones, trombone; Todd Rhodes, piano; Cuba Austin, drums; and Ralph Escudero, brass bass.

success, although he continued running bands until the late 1940s. He eventually committed suicide by hanging in 1949.

Another white band which was a nursery for young jazzmen was led by Jean Goldkette, a classically trained musician who was in fact more of a band contractor than leader. His organization controlled over 20 bands. Their output was, by and large, heavily arranged, although the imaginative Bill Challis at least accorded the soloists considerable space. The young bloods in the band included Bix Beiderbecke and Sterling Bose, trumpets; Jimmy Dorsey and Danny Polo, clarinets; Frank Trumbauer, C Melody saxophone; Tommy Dorsey and Bill Rank, trombones; Eddie Lang, guitar, and Joe Venuti, violin; in Steve Brown, from the New Orleans Rhythm Kings, they had a pounding bass

Above: Earl Hines' Grand Terrace Band, 1929. Back row: Bill Franklin, trombone; Toby Turner, clarinet and alto saxophone; Shirley Clay, trumpet; Claude Roberts, banjo and guitar; George Dixon, tenor saxophone. Front: Cecil Irwin, reeds; Hayes Alvis, brass bass; Buddy Washington, drums; George Mitchell, trumpet; Hines, piano; and Lester Boone, reeds.

Marking	Letter	Pitch	Serial Number	Matrix Number	SELECTION, COMPOSER, PUBLISHER, ETC.	Wax	Rec.	F. Cur.	Amp. Set	Level	F.
					Records by: Whitemans Orchestra						
					Chicago Lab. Nov.18th,1927. Whiteman Dir. Shields Present. Instr. 2Violin, Viola2Sax, Clarinet, Cornet,2Trombone, Bass, Guitar, Vibraphone, Bass Clarinet, (Piano By)("Hoagy" Carmichael.)						
M	CVE	100	40901	1	Washboard Blues	55-388	182	.9	3-3	40	-C
D	CVE	100	40901	2	Comp. Carmichael & Callahan	55-375	"	"	3-3	0	"
D	CVE	100	40901	3	Pub. & Copyr, J.Mills.	55-388	"	"	4-4	42	16
HC	CVE	100	40901	4	Manuscript Verbal.	55-536	"	"	4-4	42	0
D	CVE	100	40901	5	(Vocal By "Hoagy" Carmichael)	55387	"	"	4-4	42	0
					Names of Orchestra men:- Russel,Dieterle,Malineck,Jimmie Dorsey,Strickfadden, Biederback,T.Dorsey,Cullen,Brown,W.Hall,Mac Donald, C.Hazlet.						
					Time:- 9:00 To 12:15 A.M. FE. GA.						

Orchestration Changed in last 2 records.

player, who proved to be a major concern for the recording engineers.

In 1927 Paul Whiteman incorporated a large section of Goldkette's orchestra into his own, including the jazz stars to whom he gave some solo space working in the framework of Bill Challis's arrangements. By this time Whiteman had assumed his billing as the 'King of Jazz', and made a film in 1930 for Universal Pictures with that title, although the jazz content in the production was scant indeed.

Of course, Duke Ellington was more entitled to the cognomen 'King of Jazz',

but felt there was no need for such a self-regarding title – his music spoke for itself. By the end of the 1920s his orchestra was a startling ensemble of immensely talented soloists, which put together a series of outstanding recordings that, like so many other recordings of the period, have constantly reappeared in compilation form.

The coming of the big band in the 1920s set the pattern for what was to become a massive industry in the United States; at the same time these developments were having repercussions abroad – principally, initially, in Britain.

Top: The Paul Whiteman Band, 1928. Whiteman's success as a big band leader spanned the 1920s. One of the originators of the big band movement, at the start of the decade he had million-seller hits such as 'Whispering' with a nine man unit (pictured **above**, in 1919: Busse, McDonald, Johnson, Wallace, Whiteman, Caldwell, Canfield, Dornberger, and Pingitore), and claimed the title 'King of Jazz'. By the end of the 1920s, having assimilated a large part of Jean Goldkette's band, his orchestra had expanded to a phenomenal 26 members, and included such stars as Trumbauer, Beiderbecke, and the Dorsey brothers. On the information sheet (**left**) for a 1927 recording session of a Carmichael number, 'Washboard Blues', Beiderbecke's name has been incorrectly spelt.

Far left: Duke Ellington and his Famous Orchestra, 1930. Ellington's band had also increased in size. By the end of the 1930s, his was the most famous jazz orchestra in the world.

Jazz Crosses the Atlantic

Jazz had spread abroad initially via the gramophone record: the first country outside of America to receive the impact of a genuine jazz band 'live' was the United Kingdom, in April 1919, at the Hippodrome in London's West End.

The band was the Original Dixieland Jazz Band. The British public had no idea what to expect, since none of the band's records had been issued in Britain, even though they were available to the Columbia Graphophone Company (drawing from its American sister-company, Columbia), and His Master's Voice (drawing from the American label, Victor). Although an issue of the band's 'Livery Stable Blues' and 'At The Jazz Band Ball' had been mooted for the HMV label soon after it was recorded by Victor in February 1917, a stiff-necked executive at HMV decided against the issue of such a 'cacophony'.

As would be expected, reactions varied considerably once the band appeared. *Punch*, in their 16th April 1919 issue, made merry with the comment: ' "The Original Dixieland Jazz Band has arrived in London," says an evening paper. We are grateful for the warning.' One writer, in the *Performer*, wrote:

'At any rate I've come to the conclusion that the best qualification for a jazzist is to have no knowledge of music, no musical ability beyond that of making noises either on piano, or clarinet, or cornet, or trap drum, which, I believe are the proper constituents of a jazz orchestra. Of course, I may be mistaken, for I place myself among the musically uninitiated.'

Another paper, *Town Topics* wrote:

'They gave us a demonstration of undiluted jazz, and it must be admit-

ted, that despite all that has been thought and said to the contrary, there was a certain charm in the mournful refrains, dramatically broken up by cheery jingles and a miscellany of noises such as one generally hears 'off'. At one moment the whole orchestra would down tools while one member tootled merrily or eerily on his own account and the whole would resume again, always ready to give a fair hearing to any individual player who had suddenly developed a stunt.'

Encountering jazz proper for the first time – although they were not aware of this – afforded an opportunity for journalists to ask the visitors what were the origins and true meaning of the word they

Far left: The word 'jazz' reached Europe before the actual music – either 'live' or recorded – and led to much misinterpretation. Tunes such as 'When I Hear That Jazz Band Play' were pure vaudeville. Murray Pilcer's description of his group (top) as a 'jazz band' was laughably misleading – and the label on his record 'That Moaning Trombone' (above) more accurately categorizes it as a 'Comic March, One-Step'.

used to describe their new style. The *London Daily News*, 4th April 1919, reported:

'As to the word jazz, the bandsmen rejected both the current explanations. They will not have it that the word is of Red Indian origin, or that 'jazz so' is a term of praise in the dialect of the Negroes in the Southern States. The word was invented by someone in Chicago . . . It is possibly a purely onomatopoeic expression . . . In view of the unkind and disrespectful things which have been said about Red Indians and Negroids and West African savages, it should be stated that the players are all white – white as they possibly can be.'

The band's appearance was in a specially staged café scene and received a mixed ovation from the British audience but a

deafening one from a contingent of American Doughboys (servicemen) present. One person, unimpressed to the point of outrage, was the star of 'Joy Bells', George (later Sir George) Robey, who, in a seething fury, served an ultimatum to producer Albert de Courville that the Original Dixieland Jazz Band would have to go or he would leave the show. De Courville gave in and thus the first engagement of an American jazz band outside the country of its origin lasted for just one night.

However, despite this setback, or maybe because of the publicity the furore aroused, the band was booked to appear at the London Palladium shortly afterwards. An evening paper, the *Star*, commented: 'It is an interesting study to watch the faces of the dancers at the Palladium when the Original Dixieland Jazz Band,

The Melody Maker. October, 1929.

GOOD LAW
BY
GEOFFREY
CLAYTON

WHAT IS A SOUSAPHONE?

Far left, above: The Original Dixieland Jazz Band on tour. Billy Jones, piano; Larry Shields, clarinet; Nick La Rocca, cornet; Emil Christian, trombone; Tony Sbarbaro, drums. Englishman Jones replaced the original pianist, J Russell Robinson, when he returned to America , and went on to make nine recordings with the band.

Far left, below: More ephemera of the period.

Top: George Robey (right), known as 'The Prime Minister of Mirth' was a virulent critic of the Original Dixieland Jazz Band.

Above: The Hammersmith Palais, one of the venues where the Original Dixieland Jazz Band, and later Benny Peyton's Jazz Kings, had so much success.

Top: The Original Lyrical Five, 1923. A British band that emulated The Original Dixieland Jazz Band and played at the Hammersmith Palais. The clarinettist is Harry Roy, with his brother Syd at the piano and Lew Davis on trombone. The Original Lyrical Five was a short-lived band. Davis became Britain's first recognized jazz trombonist in Lew Stone's Orchestra in the 1930s, and Harry Roy became a famous band leader in his own right.

Below: Lew Davis seen later in his long and distinguished career.

which is said to be the only one of its kind in the world, is doing its best to murder music.'

Encore was also highly critical:

'I once heard of a man who jumped from a ten-storey building and dashed his brains out. He caused a sensation. President Wilson has departed. Jazz has arrived. I do not know which is having the worst effect. In this act there is a piano, trap drummer, flageolet [sic], cornet, trombone and male and female dancers. After what seems to one like loud rolls of dreadful thunder a girl dressed in a half-green muff sang to a discordant row 'Wonderful Smile'.

It is wonderful what the world is coming to. The lady is indeed clever, for she danced without moving her feet – in fact, when she danced with her partner she was more danced against than dancing. After her departure a man came in and wiggled himself about like a filleted eel about to enter the stewing pot. This is the most discordant and uninteresting entertainment I have ever seen at the Palladium.'

After seeing jazz, musical studies are of no account. I can see clearly that if I can rattle on any old tin my future is made.'

The band stayed in Britain for 15 months playing different venues and they were received at Buckingham Palace by King George V and Queen Mary. There, according to leader La Rocca, they were scrutinized by a gathering of British nobility who 'peered at us as though we had bugs on us'. They opened up with a steaming version of their most famous tune, 'Tiger Rag', and the audience were petrified, some glancing uneasily at the nearest exit. At the conclusion of the number there was an embarrassing silence until King George laughed his approval and began to applaud energetically, his approval quickly taken up by the entourage.

The band departed England in July 1920, after a very successful visit (despite George Robey), but their departure was not without some anxiety for La Rocca. The band had been a big hit among the 'Bright Young Things' of the British aristocracy, the behaviour and the dress of the females particularly reflecting the

ROYAL ENTERTAINMENT.

CHAT WITH CRIMEAN VETERAN

In the grounds of Buckingham Palace on Saturday the King and Queen gave a happy time to over eleven hundred guests, mainly the servants of the various departments of the Royal household, their wives, and children. The Palace police and their families were invited, as were all the workers in and about the Royal residence. The King and Queen were accompanied by Princess Mary, Prince Albert, Queen Alexandra, the Empress Marie of Russia, Princess Victoria, and Prince Waldemar of Denmark. The band of the Royal Horse Guards supplied music during the afternoon, and there were performances also by the Southern Syncopated Orchestra from the Philharmonic Hall and by a Nigger Jazz Band. All the arrangements were made by Mr. George Ashton, their Majesties' theatrical agent; and by the Queen's special wish particular attention was devoted to the entertainment of the children.

The proceedings began with a concert and

born in barracks in 1837. His father was a rifleman in the Rifle Brigade, and at three years of age he went with him to Corfu, in the Mediterranean. In 1850 he returned to England, enlisted in the Army three years later, and was discharged in 1858. He went to the Crimea in 1856, practically at the end of the campaign. The King noticed that though the old soldier was wearing many decorations, the Crimean medal was not among them, and the sergeant explained, with a twinkle in his eye, that he took no part in the actual fighting, and that medals were not won so easily on that occasion as on some others. He also served against the Fenians in Canada.

Below the programme is set out, with the exception of the improvised additions made for the entertainment of the children:

Wilkin and McGowan, living marionettes; Frank Whitman, the dancing violinist; song, "Swing Along," by the Philharmonic company; song, "Jessamina," Messrs. McKinney, Payne, Rosemund, and Williams; song, "I got a Robe," Carroll Morgan; songs, "Mother o' Mine" and "Peaches Down in Georgia," by Messrs. McKinney, Payne, Rosemund, and Williams; a comic lecture, "Exhortation," by Joe Porter; song, "Me, O Lord," by Messrs. McKinney, Payne, Rosemund, and Williams; accompanist, Will Marion Cook; bandoline, Lawrence Morris; clarinet, Sydney Bechet; cornet, William Briggs; trombone, William Forrester; drums, Robert Young; Conan, the ventriloquist. Interval for tea. After tea, Punch and Judy performance and a musical clown

Above: Benny Peyton's Jazz Kings (a contingent from the Southern Syncopated Orchestra), c.1920. Seated on the far right is Sidney Bechet, whose sullen look is no doubt caused by the rather outrageous costume he had to wear. Bechet had more serious things to worry about during his visit to Britain: he was arrested on a rape charge, and, although acquitted, his stay was brought to a halt by deportation.

Left: Reproduced from the London *Times* of 11th August 1919, this Court Circular records, in the language of the day, the appearance before their Majesties of 'a Nigger Jazz Band' – the Southern Syncopated Orchestra. Bechet is mentioned by name. To put the general attitude to jazz at the time in perspective, the band was given equal billing with a Punch and Judy show.

Above: The Mound City Blue Blowers. Dick Slevin, kazoo; Jack Bland, banjo; Eddie Lang, guitar; and Red McKenzie, comb and paper. Following the success of their record, 'Arkansas Blues', the band toured Britain in 1924. Their engagements included East End music halls and a stint at the elite Piccadilly Grill. Guitarist Eddie Lang had a most varied career, recording with individuals as disparate in style and background as Bessie Smith 'Empress of the Blues', Bix Beiderbecke, King Oliver, Joe Venuti, Paul Whiteman, Bing Crosby and Jack Teagarden. He died, following a tonsilectomy operation, in 1933.

changes in manners and morals a long war had brought about. The story goes that Lord Harrington, the outraged father of a beautiful debutante who had been consorting with La Rocca, chased La Rocca down to Southampton Docks with a loaded shotgun. Later, La Rocca alleged he had been lucky to get out of England alive.

The band's trombonist, Emil Christian, stayed in Britain and organized a band to cash in on the Original Dixieland Jazz Band's popularity and wrote to La Rocca asking for his help in obtaining suitable musicians. He added in a letter: 'And Joe, take a tip from me. From what I understand old man Harrington is going to fill you full of lead if you ever set foot in England again. So be careful and watch yourself if you ever come back'.

The first big coloured orchestra to play in Britain was Will Marion Cook's Southern Syncopated Orchestra. It contained one genuine jazzman, the Creole clarinettist Sidney Bechet. Bechet's play-

ing made a tremendous impression on the conductor of L'Orchestre de la Suisse Romande, Ernest Ansermet, who wrote a glowing review in the *Review Romande*, 19th October 1919, after hearing Bechet with the orchestra in London, thus making Ansermet virtually the first jazz 'critic'. Other writers were equally enthusiastic, if not so perceptive. A reviewer in the *Daily Herald* referred to 'real ragtime by real darkies', an allusion to the blacked-up white performers of so-called ragtime who had been a feature of the music halls since the turn of the century.

Various white American bands, with virtually no jazz content, like Paul Whiteman's and Paul Specht's, appeared in Britain, and in addition a trickle of genuine recordings haphazardly began to enter the catalogues. One such was by Lizzie Miles from New Orleans singing 'My Pillow And Me' and 'Black Man, Be On Your Way'. Considering the suggestive nature of the lyrics and her earthy diction this issue must have mystified what

Record Labels

Albeit erratically, genuine jazz recordings began to find their way into the British catalogues. These included one by the New Orleans blues singer, Lizzie Miles; the classic 'Black Bottom Stomp' (advertized as a Charleston) by 'Jelly Roll' Morton's Red Hot Peppers; and various Fletcher Henderson recordings, usually – as in the case of the 'Corona Dance Orchestra' – under pseudonyms.

THE MELODY MAKER.   9

SYNCOPATION AND DANCE BAND NEWS.

PAUL WHITEMAN and his SYMPHONIC SYNCOPATED CONCERT ORCHESTRA.

Paul Whiteman for England.

We learn that arrangements are nearing completion for the visit to this country in the early Spring of Paul Whiteman who, with his Symphonic Syncopated Concert Orchestra, will give a number of concerts, probably twenty in all, throughout London and the provinces.

As will be seen from the above photograph, which is of Whiteman's Orchestra as it will actually appear in England, the combination is twenty-seven strong, not counting Whiteman himself, and very different to that with which he appeared at the London Hippodrome in 1923.

Whereas in London Paul Whiteman will be represented by Messrs. Lionel Powell & Holt, in America he is now, and has been since last season, under the direction of William Morris, who was also agent to Harry Lauder.

The Canadian Club Band.

Paul Specht's Canadian Club Orchestra, led by Orville Johnson, which recently arrived from Canada on the "Majestic," is now playing at the Kit Cat Club, London, and proving a great success.

A ten-piece combination, its members, who are all Canadians, between them account for thirty-five different instruments. There are three vocalists in the outfit, and the leader can sing and extemporize on the spur of the moment a song about anyone or anything he notices. Among them is also a good ballad singer and a very clever "rag" singer. Art Christmas, the first trumpet, is also a red-hot "dirt" sax. player, and the whole crowd is about as lively a bunch as one could wish for.

Left: Paul Whiteman visited Britain in 1923 and 1926. On the second visit the orchestra, as detailed in the *Melody Maker*, was to total 28, including Whiteman himself. The *Melody Maker* cutting also features Paul Specht's Canadian Club Orchestra. Earlier, a contingent of Dixielanders in Specht's band, called The Georgians, had recorded 'Snakes Hips' under the pseudonym of the Regal Novelty Orchestra (**above**).

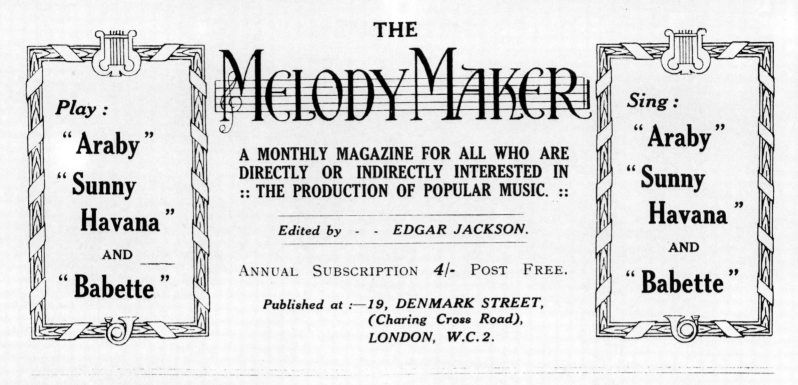

THE
Melody Maker

A MONTHLY MAGAZINE FOR ALL WHO ARE
DIRECTLY OR INDIRECTLY INTERESTED IN
:: THE PRODUCTION OF POPULAR MUSIC. ::

Edited by - - EDGAR JACKSON.

ANNUAL SUBSCRIPTION **4/-** POST FREE.

*Published at :—19, DENMARK STREET,
(Charing Cross Road),
LONDON, W.C.2.*

Play :

"**Araby**"

"**Sunny
Havana**"

AND

"**Babette**"

Sing :

"**Araby**"

"**Sunny
Havana**"

AND

"**Babette**"

No. 1.   Vol. I.   JANUARY 1926.   PRICE **3**d.

The Melody Maker

EDITORIAL TELEPHONE - REGENT 4147.

*Members of the Profession and all others are Cordially
Invited to submit MSS. Information and Photographs
for Publication.*

*** Whereas every care is taken, we cannot be responsible
for the loss of any matter submitted.

Stamped and addressed envelope should be enclosed if
return of any matter submitted is desired.

**RATES FOR ADVERTISING SPACE
WILL BE SENT ON REQUEST.**

INDEX.

Editorial	1
Over The Footlights	2
Syncopation and Dance Band News ...	7
The Prophets of Doom, by Jack Hylton ...	14
MY GIRL'S GOT LONG HAIR, Song ...	16
Gramophone Record Making, by Percival Mackey	18
The Banjo in Modern Dance Orchestra, by Emile Grimshaw	22
How To Read Music At Sight, by Hubert Bath	24
About Ukuleles, by Kel Keech ...	26
America's Idea of English Jazz	27
Military and Brass Band News	28
The Gramophone Review	31

EDITORIAL.

It is usual, we believe, when introducing a new
publication, to say a few words before the curtain
as it were. Whereas we do not propose after this
to adhere to any example already set by others,
but rather to branch out for ourselves in our own
way, we feel it due to our readers to give briefly
the *raison d'etre* of our existence.

We must confess that we have, on more occasions
than we like to admit, noticed a lack of co-ordina-
tion between the many branches of the entertainment profession, when the closest co-operation
ought, in the interests of all concerned, to have
existed.

Which brings us to our point. By giving in an
interesting manner, between these two covers, up-
to-date information of as many branches of popular
entertainment as space will permit, we hope to
let each section know exactly on what the other is
concentrating, so that concerted efforts may
enhance the success of all.

If we succeed in only a small measure we shall
feel our humble effort has not been made in vain.

We have decided to devote our frontispiece
each month to some prominent member of the
musical profession.

In this, our first issue, we are indebted to the
famous British composer, Mr. Horatio Nicholls,
for allowing us the privilege of publishing his
photograph.

Born in Leicester, Mr. Nicholls rapidly came
to the fore and is now admittedly one of the
finest and most popular composers of lighter
music, not only in England, but throughout the
world.

THE EDITOR.

Above: One of Jackson's other activities before founding the world's first jazz journal was performing in a variety hall dog act.

Above: Edgar Jackson, founder and first editor of the *Melody Maker*, with an unknown dancing partner. Before turning to publishing, ex-army officer Jackson earned his living as a professional dancer.

Left: Frontispiece of the first issue of the *Melody Maker*. January 1926. This was the first journal in the world to give serious (if, perhaps understandably, ill-informed) coverage to jazz. It continued its support of the idiom until the early 1980s, when it switched emphasis entirely onto the various manifestations of rock 'n' roll.

very few purchasers there were.

Many of the recordings were issued under pseudonyms, usually because the companies deemed the new names to be more appealing than the original ones, though it is doubtful whether the British public at that time would have been any wiser had they known the real identities. An example was the series of recordings by Fletcher Henderson's Orchestra, some containing brief, flaring passages by Louis Armstrong, released under a false name: more than likely listeners objected to this 'hot' departure from the melody, unconcerned about the identity of the performer. However, one label, Imperial,

in 1925, issued a recording by Fletcher Henderson under his own name which contained Louis Armstrong's first ever vocal on gramophone record. It was 'Everybody Loves My Baby' and Armstrong could be heard uttering a few words of what must have seemed gibberish at the time.

In 1926 a classic jazz recording, 'Black Bottom Stomp' and 'The Chant' by 'Jelly Roll' Morton's Red Hot Peppers, was issued on the HMV label. The spirited solo and collective improvization was well served by the new electrical recording method, a vast improvement on the old muddy sound of the acoustic process.

Jazz criticism in America and elsewhere was almost non-existent in the sense of the music's intrinsic qualities being recognized and analyzed; indeed, most of the reportage was akin to that received by the Original Dixieland Jazz Band. Perhaps surprisingly, considering the alleged conservatism of the British character, Britain was the first country to produce a regular magazine that was to treat jazz music seriously. This paper was the

The Problems of an Immodest Masterpiece

THERE are doubtless many who, while admiring the technique of this year's problem picture, by John B. Soutar, will affect to be able to interpret this pictorial metaphor as a further slap in the face for modern dancing and its particular type of music.

We will impugn no discreditable motive to the artist, but, on the other hand, will freely admit that he was surely animated with the highest artistic motives when he composed this work. The hanging committee of the Royal Academy, too, with its usual dispassionate disregard for subject, will have viewed it only for its artistic merit—that is to say, on its quality as a work of art alone. All the same, speaking as we do for dance musicians in this country, we object to this picture because of the inferences it is capable of bearing to the many others who may view it less than a work of art and more as a sermon.

We jazz musicians are not thin-skinned, fortunately, for we are subjected, by those who know less than nothing about us, to the most bitter and illogical criticisms of this generation, but this picture bears such possible alternative interpretations as to be positively indecent. Those who bear us ill-will will undoubtedly interpret it in this wrongful manner.

THE BREAKDOWN .. .. John B. Soutar.

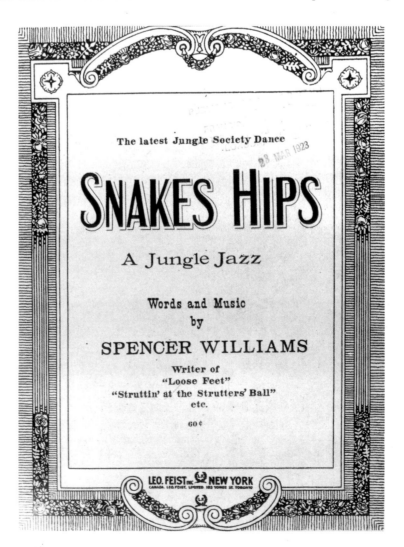

(Copyright reserved for owner by Walter Judd, Ltd.)

It is not our intention to labour the point, and so to give this picture a publicity disproportionate to its value, but we state emphatically that we protest against, and repudiate the juxtaposition of an undraped white girl with a black man. Such a study is straining beyond breaking point the normal clean inferences of allegory. We demand also that the habit of associating our music with the primitive and barbarous negro derivation shall cease forthwith, in justice to the obvious fact that we have outgrown such comparison.

Problem pictures are capable, we reiterate, of a thousand and one different and antipodal interpretations. The artist visualises one and every thinking spectator visualises another ; rarely can they be reconciled. In this case we will extract what comfort we can from this indelicate creation by interpreting for ourselves the only suggestion of a conventional and fair allegory which appears to us in the whole picture.

We see Minerva lying shattered and neglected in the background. It is said that, for the purpose of this picture, she represented the "old order of things" which the iconoclasm of jazz has hewn down. Minerva, however,

(Continued on page 3, col. 3)

Melody Maker, and first appeared in January 1926, financed by a music publisher, Lawrence Wright, who composed songs under the pseudonym of Horatio Nicholls. Its founder and editor was Edgar Jackson, an ex-army officer, who had previously been a variety-hall artiste in a dog act, and a professional dancer. The paper announced itself as 'a monthly magazine for all directly or indirectly interested in the production of popular music' and its contents were primarily aimed at the dance band industry that was flourishing in Britain at the time, which was seen as a good potential source of advertizing revenue.

The first mention of a 'jazz musician' concerned violinist Hugo Rignold, later conductor, at various times, of the Palestine Symphony Orchestra, the Sadlers Wells Ballet Company, the Liverpool Philharmonic Orchestra, the City of Birmingham Symphony Orchestra and the Cape Town Symphony Orchestra. The review quaintly observed that he was 'leading a band at Kettners Hotel, Church Street [now Romilly Street], Soho, a

Above: 'The Breakdown', a painting by John B. Soutar. Edgar Jackson and the *Melody Maker* were involved in a great controversy when Jackson, in a fierce editorial, strongly objected to the portrayal of a naked ('undraped') white girl with a black musician. At the request of the Colonial office the painting was withdrawn from the Royal Academy's catalogue, and from its walls, in 1926. It seemed that Jackson wished to dissociate 'our music' from 'the primitive and barbarous negro derivation . . . in justice to the obvious fact that we have outgrown such comparison.'

Left and right: Song-sheet covers of the period, again reflecting the confused racial attitudes prevailing at the time. 'Snakes Hips' is promoted as a 'jungle' jazz, while 'Hot Lips', which was, in fact, one of the feature numbers of Paul Whiteman's Orchestra on their visit to Britain, was publicized by Francis, Day & Hunter with a caricature of a pop-eyed black man, struggling to produce a note: Henry Busse, the trumpeter who actually played the tune, was, of course, white.

The latest Jungle Society Dance

SNAKES HIPS

A Jungle Jazz

Words and Music by

SPENCER WILLIAMS

Writer of
"Loose Feet"
"Struttin' at the Strutters' Ball"
etc.

60¢

LEO. FEIST inc. NEW YORK

famous landmark which achieved the height of its popularity in the days of King Edward VII, who, rumour has it, was very partial to the secluded and select spot. Lunch and dinner are served, as in the old days unaccompanied by aught else but the tinkle of plate and glass and the subdued laughter of the elite of London's society'.

Rignold was also mentioned as playing 'real dirt' on the fiddle in a record, 'Riverboat Shuffle', by Jack Hylton's Kit Kat Band. The *Melody Maker*'s reviewer Edgar Jackson gave coverage to the jazz records being released, but, as there were no histories, biographies, autobiographies, or discographies then, Jackson was constantly in the dark. He objected strongly to the crudities he perceived in black jazz, and the combination of his understandable ignorance, and less acceptable colour prejudice, amounted to reviews that were often quite hilarious – but it was at least a beginning in the exercise of structured jazz appreciation.

In a review of 'Black Bottom Stomp' and 'The Chant' by 'Jelly Roll' Morton, Jackson wrote: 'None can say that the musicians are not wonderful performers. Nevertheless, you are treated to an exhibition of the bluest jazz, not as it should be today, but as it was six years ago. The fact that this is about the best record I have come across for Charleston dancing owing to the 'hot' rhythm behind it certainly does not excuse the fact that it is crude in orchestration and poor amusement to listen to.' He was rather prone to such references as 'niggers', 'darkies' and 'coons' – astonishingly, quite normal language for a magazine in the 1920s, even coming from Britain's foremost contemporary authority on an idiom

Above, right, and far right: Typical *Melody Maker* advertisements of the time. Of most interest is the advertisement on the opposite page from the May 1928 issue, promoting the historic launch by Parlophone of their famous 'Rhythm-Style' series of recordings. These were the first planned jazz releases in Europe, and were drawn from the American OKEH label. Not even the advertizers knew that the cornettist (not trumpeter) on the Trumbauer titles was the legendary Bix Beiderbecke – one of the immortal figures of jazz. The advertisement at the top of this page is for Bert Firman's Rhythmic Eight: was Firman so well-known that his name could be safely omitted?

PARLOPHONE
NEW RECORDS OF MODERN DANCE MUSIC.
ALL 10-inch BLUE LABEL RECORDS, 3/- EACH

FRANKIE TRUMBAUER
King of all Saxophone Players
and the greatest figure in
Modern Music.

MIFF MOLE
The world's greatest Trombone
Player and the most brilliant
creator of modern music phrasing

HAVE YOU HEARD
THE NEW WONDER RECORD BY
FRANKIE TRUMBAUER
AND HIS MARVELLOUS ORCHESTRA
FEATURING
THE RHYTHM BOYS.

R 3526 | MISSISSIPPI MUD, Fox-Trot
| THERE'LL COME A TIME, Fox-Trot

FRANKIE TRUMBAUER has made another wonderful record, this time he introduces the famous RHYTHM BOYS. "Mississippi Mud" a tune in a thousand, will be a great popular favourite with all followers of this outstanding Orchestra. In "There'll Come a Time" FRANKIE TRUMBAUER'S chorus is at his very best, never before have such marvellous breaks for saxophone and trumpet been heard as on this side. Listen to the double break by the trumpet in the trumpet chorus, and to the final sax break by Frankie Trumbauer just before the coda. Note here how the last two notes of this break are miraculously taken up by the trumpet from Trumbauer playing sax.

MIFF MOLE'S LITTLE MOLERS
— with *MIFF MOLE Himself* —
THE REAL HOT-TIME ORCHESTRA.

R 3530 | ORIGINAL DIXIELAND, One-Step
| MY GAL SAL, Fox-Trot

MIFF MOLE and his LITTLE MOLERS need no introduction. They are old favourites. MIFF MOLE is the greatest trombone player in the world, and the originator of more hot breaks and new phrases than any other dance artiste. He has certainly made a dance record all appreciators of hot records will enjoy. ADRIAN ROLLINI puts in some strong work on both sides of this record.

EXCLUSIVE ON PARLOPHONE

Insist on hearing these wonderful Records at your nearest stores or dealers. In case of difficulty apply to
THE PARLOPHONE COMPANY, LTD., 85, CITY ROAD, LONDON, E.C.1

which had so clearly arisen from a black culture.

These stumbling excursions into jazz criticism reflected the beginning of a specialized interest in jazz in the UK, which soon prompted the release of the first ever consciously planned series of jazz recordings by an English record company. This was Parlophone, and the recordings were called the 'Rhythm-style' series. They drew upon a treasury of jazz recordings from the American OKEH label that included Louis Armstrong's Hot Five and Hot Seven, Duke Ellington's Orchestra, Frankie Trumbauer's Orchestra with Bix Beiderbecke, Bix Beiderbecke and his Gang, Miff Mole and his Molers, Joe Venuti and Eddie Lang, and many others.

A band that Jackson praised highly was that led by the pianist and composer Fred (Federico) Elizalde from Manila, in the Philippines. Elizalde had formed the 'Quinquaginta Ramblers', an undergraduate jazz band, at Cambridge in 1927, who recorded for the Brunswick label. On turning professional, Elizalde led an Anglo-American band which included the multi-instrumentalist Adrian Rollini; based at the Savoy Hotel in the Strand, London, they too recorded for Brunswick.

Bert Firman's Rhythmic Eight on the Zonophone Label included much improvization in their arrangements, but these were not specifically advertised as jazz recordings. The first to create such a series in the United Kingdom was the Anglo-Irishman Spike Hughes with his Decca-Dents – later 'Dance Orchestra' – on the Decca label. The players were all

Above: Typical cardboard 78rpm record sleeves of the 1920s. For some reason it was a fact of the retail trade that cycles were stocked alongside gramophones, their accessories, and records. The 'Songster' steel needles ('Soft, Loud, or Medium') were inserted into heavy tone arms that gouged the surface of the shellac. Early collectors may have chanced upon gems in such mundane outlets, but for the more discerning enthusiast Levy's Record Shop (**top**), in London's Whitechapel, held a stock of 'hot' records, and proudly advertized the fact. They were the first British retailer to specialize in jazz, and even started their own labels, Levaphone and Oriole.

JAZZ AT THE SAVOY

ARKANSAS · DIXIE · HURRICANE · SUGAR STEP · SOMEBODY STOLE MY GAL

THE DARKTOWN STRUTTERS' BALL · CLARINET MARMALADE · SUGAR · STOMP YOUR FEET · TIGER RAG

FRED ELIZALDE and his **Orchestra**

DECCA RECORDS
TRUE HIGH FIDELITY
LONG PLAYING 33⅓ R.P.M. RECORD
LF 1277

Above: Fred Elizalde and his Anglo-American Band at the Savoy Hotel. Dick Maxwell, vocals; Len Fillis, guitar; Adrian Rollini, bass saxophone; Ronnie Gubertini, drums; Rex Owen, tenor saxophone; Norman Payne, trumpet; Chelsea Quealey, trumpet; Harry Hayes, alto saxophone; Bobby Davis, clarinet and alto saxophone.

Right: Fred Elizalde was the son of a rich Manillan sugar magnate: before he set up the Anglo-American Band he had founded and led the Quinquaginta Ramblers at Cambridge University.

Above: Bert Firman, leader of Bert Firman's Rhythm Eight. Many British dance bands tried to play jazz, with varying degrees of success. Along with the Savoy Orpheans and Jack Hylton's Band, the Rhythm Eight were among the best.

professional dance band musicians with a leaning towards jazz, and the recordings stand as a testament to a genuine pioneering spirit. Spike Hughes later became the chronicler of the Glyndebourne Festivals, and lost interest in jazz.

In 1930 the 'High-Hatted Tragedian of Jazz', clarinettist/singer Ted Lewis,

Above: The Savoy Hotel in the Strand, the glass facia of which can just be seen on the left of the picture, was a haunt of the well-to-do, but, surprisingly, retained Fred Elizalde and his jazz musicians and was to become an important location for British jazz in the 1920s and 1930s. Elizalde specially imported American jazzmen Chelsea Quealy, Bobby Davis, and Adrian Rollini.

Left: Spike Hughes was a key figure in British jazz in the late 1920s and early 1930s. Bassist, composer, and arranger, his recordings with the Decca-Dents — the first records created by British artistes to be advertized as 'jazz' — did much to transform the way that the idiom was viewed in the United Kingdom when they were issued between 1930 and 1932.

A JAZZ HOLIDAY

Ted Lewis

AND HIS BAND

ONE OF
AMERICA'S
TOP BANDS OF
THE 20'S

ASV
LIVING ERA

brought a band to play at a London restaurant which included trumpeter Muggsy Spanier, trombonist George Lewis, and clarinettist Jimmy Dorsey, all to be hallowed in the jazz pantheon, but whose talents were largely subservient to the posturing Lewis on this tour. It was not until 1932 that Britain welcomed a genuine giant of jazz, Louis Armstrong.

Throughout the 1920s music of all kinds continued to be falsely described as jazz, but a vein of the real thing existed throughout the decade, either in the issue of genuine jazz recordings, or in local performances after British musicians had thoroughly analyzed them; by then, too, the foundation for more enlightened technical and artistic appreciation was being laid by the *Melody Maker*.

Left: Ephemera of the period. 'Gramophone Review' was an important feature of *The Melody Maker*.

Above: Ted Lewis, 'The High-Hatted Tragedian of Jazz', visited Britain in 1926 and 1930. He played the clarinet in a grotesque 'gas-pipe' style, postured in an extrovert burlesque manner, and sang in a pseudo-dramatic recitative style. His saving grace was that he employed many fine jazzmen, including trumpeter Muggsy Spanier; trombonist George Brunies; and clarinettist Jimmy Dorsey; all of whom were with him on the 1930 tour.

Above: Django Reinhardt, born in Belgium on 23rd January 1910. His family were travelling entertainers, and in his childhood he toured around Belgium and France with them, learning to play the violin and guitar as he went.

Left: Europe meets America: Django working on an arrangement with Duke Ellington.

Below left: Record sleeve for 'House of Dreams', a Reinhardt composition, recorded with the Quintet of the Hot Club of France.

Vogue EPV 1208

DJANGO REINHARDT

In Europe jazz activity was considerable in France, Holland, Denmark and Sweden. The top French bands featuring jazz musicians were Gregor and his Gregorians and Ray Ventura's Collegians; the foremost soloists were violinist Stephane Grappelli, trombonist Leo Vauchant, trumpeter Philip Brun, tenor saxophonists Andre Ekyan, and Philip Combelle. The most outstanding – and certainly Europe's finest contribution to jazz – was the gypsy guitarist Django Reinhardt. Actually, Reinhardt was born in a caravan, in Liberchies, near Luttre in Belgium, on 23rd January 1910, but it was said of him that 'home is where he happened to be' and sometime in the 1920s the Reinhardts pitched their caravan in a gypsy settlement outside Paris. He was a founder member of the most famous of all French jazz units, the Quintette du Hot Club de France, sharing the solos with Stephan Grappelly (as his name was then spelt). They made over 200 recordings, each displaying Reinhardt's staggering technique and wealth

mono ACL 1158

Django **REINHARDT** Stephane **Grappelly**
with
The Quintet of the Hot Club of France

ace
of
clubs
Treasury SERIES

Honeysuckle Rose   Night and Day   Sweet Georgia Brown   Love's Melody
Nuages   Daphne   Liza   Belleville   Souvenirs   My Sweet

of invention, all the more astonishing as he had lost two fingers of his left hand in a caravan fire in 1928. Reinhardt recorded with several black musicians who found the racial and social climate in France more acceptable than at home, these including alto saxophonist Benny Carter, tenor saxophonist Coleman Hawkins, trombonist Dickie Wells, and trumpeter Bill Coleman.

France produced two outstanding critics in Charles Delaunay and Hughes

Above: The Quintet of the Hot Club of France. Stephane Grappelli, violin; Eugene Vees, guitar; Emmanuel Soudieux (standing), bass; Django Reinhardt; Joseph Reinhardt, guitar. Django Reinhardt was the group's central focus — recognized from very early in his career as a genius. After playing in the bars of Paris as a soloist, he worked as an accompanist, before founding the quintet with Stephane Grappelli. The band soon achieved success, and named itself after the record and concert society which promoted them.

Grappelli, though often overshadowed by Reinhardt, is one of the other great names of European jazz. He was born in Paris on 26th January 1908, and studied both the piano and the violin at the Paris Conservatoire during his teens. Reinhardt died tragically young at 43, but Grappelli continued a long and highly distinguished career, enjoying enormous popularity, especially in the 1970s with a quartet featuring Diz Disley on guitar.

HAIL BECHET !

ON HIS WAY to the "Hot Club" to hear the result of Wilcox's negotiations for his proposed trip to England, Sidney Bechet poses for **JAZZ ILLUSTRATED** photographer in the Rue Bechet. Each of the numerous alleyways surrounding the "Hot Club of Paris" is named after a famous jazz-man.

...and Bechet played

MAY, 1949 and the Paris Jazz Festival. Hot Lips Page, Sidney Bechet, Charlie Parker, Tad Dameron, were among the host of American stars that had 500 British jazz fans trekking to that part of the world, knowing, that in consequence of the Musicians' Union's ban, there would be precious little chance of ever hearing these greats of jazz in a British Festival.

Came October 1949 and a return visit of that Grand Old Man of New Orleans jazz, Sidney Bechet, to take part in a series of concerts throughout Europe, with the exception of Britain, of course. But with the sympathy of every jazz fan in the country and the weight of the N.F.J.O. behind them, the Wilcox Organisation set the wheels in motion in a determined effort to present Bechet to the jazz starved British fans in a series of six concerts in London and the provinces.

Immediate application to the M.U. for a permit allowing Bechet to play here was, after some weeks delay, flatly refused. Their reason being the old and sorry one of non-reciprocity on the part of the American Union.

A further application made to the V.A.F. resulted in a ray of hope, that broadminded body giving the proposition their full blessing. The final say in the matter, however, rested with the Ministry of Labour. But not until the 14th November, two days before Bechet returned to America did they have their say. It was NO.

A week before this decision was made known, Bert Wilcox, over in Paris taking in the Armstrong concert and reporting the progress of the Organisation's negotiations to Bechet's agent, renewed his acquaintance with Sidney Bechet and invited the veteran clarinet player to spend the week-end in London as his guest. In the ensuing pages **JAZZ ILLUSTRATED** tells you the story of those now memorable 48 hours.

THE UNION IMPOSE A BAN ON BECHET

IT WAS A STORY of failure that Bert Wilcox had to report to Bechet, and agent Charles Delaunay. The three men found the attitude of the Union very difficult to understand in view of the fact that Bechet, a solo artist, would have created work for British musicians. A viewpoint that 100,000 British fans also share. Jazz lovers would also like to know why Anton Karas, the man with the zither, also a foreign musician, is granted a six week contract to play in this country, whilst the ban is put up to Bechet and other jazz musicians

6

Panassiè: Delaunay compiling the first jazz discography, *Hot Discography*, entering the operative word into the language. He founded the 'Swing" label and promoted the Quintette du Hot Club de France. Panassiè wrote the first serious book on jazz, *Le Jazz Hot* (1934), edited *Jazz Hot* and organized the New York recording sessions with clarinettist Mezz Mezzrow, trumpeter Tommy Ladnier and soprano saxophonist Sidney Bechet. In the 1930s Delaunay and Panassiè were close friends, but during the war Panassiè went to live in Vichy France, and Delaunay stayed in Paris and was involved in the Resistance movement. Panassiè totally rejected bop, whereas Delaunay embraced it – so the one-time friends fell out, never to be reconciled.

In Holland the leading band was the Ramblers, led by pianist Theo Uden Masman. They accompanied Benny Carter, Coleman Hawkins and singer Connie Boswell on recording sessions. A popular figure was Louis de Vries, a Louis Armstrong imitator, who for some circumlocutory reason was known as the 'Dutch Nat Gonella'. He toured English variety halls as a solo act.

Joost van Praag and Hank Neisen were two influential Dutch critics, and Boy ten Hoven was an outstanding caricaturist.

Scandinavia welcomed Louis Armstrong in 1933, playing at Tivoli, Copenhagen, on 19th October, and at the Auditorium Concert Hall, Stockholm, on 24th October; the last concert recorded via the Swedish State Telephone Company. An astute engineer linked the equipment to an acetate machine and, although badly recorded, gave us some of the few examples of Louis Armstrong with the indifferent pick-up band (recruited from Paris cafés) that accompanied him on his Scandinavian trip.

In Copenhagen, the Armstrong concert would have almost certainly been attended by bandleader alto saxophonist Kai Ewans and by violinist Svend Asmussen; and in Stockholm, trumpeter bandleader Thore Ehrling would have been in the audience.

The recordings of the Ewans and Ehrling bands exhibit a high technical standard and included many fine soloists. Both were very successful backing the consummate musician Benny Carter. There was also some jazz activity in Germany, Switzerland, Belgium and Norway, revealing the extent to which jazz had become an international language by the mid-1930s.

Left: A contemporary report from *Jazz Illustrated* makes a fascinating comparison between British and Continental attitudes at the time. The article lists American stars Bechet, 'Hot Lips' Page, Charlie Parker, and Tadd Dameron as participants in the 1949 Paris Jazz Festival, while at the time all were prevented from performing in Britain because of a ban on foreign musicians instigated by a protective Musician's Union. Seen in the lower picture with Bert Wilcox, the British impresario, and Bechet, is Charles Delaunay, one of the most influential figures in Continental jazz history. To complete the story of 'those now memorable 48 hours' that Bechet spent in Britain as the guest of the Wilcox brothers turn to page 115.

Top: Hughes Panassiè, President of the Hot Club of France, welcomes Earl Hines and Velma Middleton to Paris. Another hugely influential figure, Panassiè was a bitter rival of Delaunay over the traditional versus modernist debate.

Above: Louis de Vries and his Royal Orpheans, 1931. The picture was taken during a tour of Holland and Germany. The band was highly cosmopolitan in its composition, including star names Eddie Breunner (Swiss), Freddy Schweitzer (German), Mick Amstell (British), and Melle Weersma (Dutch). De Vries made a successful tour of Britain in 1935, and recorded several numbers for the Decca label.

Swing Fever

The geneaology of what became known as the swing band can be traced onwards from the Fletcher Henderson band to the Jean Goldkette unit. There is then a strong connection between Goldkette and the Casa Loma Orchestra – generally referred to as the first of the swing bands. The Casa Loma commenced business at the Greystone Ballroom, Detroit, where Goldkette had been in residence. Like all the big white bands that followed in their train, their repertoire inevitably consisted largely of the popular tunes of the day played 'straight' with heavy emphasis on vocals, while featuring 'spot' numbers with a greater element of improvization.

Tenor saxophonist/playboy Charlie Barnet was one of the first to form a new band in this style, but infinitely better known were the Dorsey brothers, Jimmy (alto saxophone and clarinet), and Tommy (trombone and trumpet). They were soon known as the 'feuding brothers', constantly fighting, both musically, and, sometimes, physically. In 1935, each formed his own orchestra and became commercially successful with a standard mix of ballads and jazz features in their repertoire. Both were to have million-seller hits – Tommy in 1937 with 'Marie', in 1938 with 'Boogie Woogie', and in 1942 with 'There Are Such Things' (with Frank Sinatra and the Pied Pipers); and Jimmy in 1941 with 'Amapola', in 1943 with 'Besame Mucho' (Kiss Me), and in 1957 with 'So Rare'.

The first big success story of the swing era belongs to the Chicagoan clarinettist Benny Goodman. Superficially a rather unprepossessing man, who did not appear to have the makings of a successful pop music figure, he was a jazzman at heart (like the Dorseys), and included as much

Above, left: The Casa Loma Orchestra. This was regarded as the first of the 'swing' orchestras, featuring orchestrations of jazz tunes, like 'China Boy' many composed and arranged by guitarist Gene Gifford.

Left: Charlie Barnet, tenor and soprano saxophonist, known as the 'Mad Mab', was a well heeled playboy, who was married eight times. He formed his first band in 1934, and maintained a high jazz content throughout over two decades as a band leader.

Above: The Dorsey brothers, Tommy (left), who played the trombone and trumpet, and Jimmy, who played the trumpet, clarinet, and alto saxophone, featured on countless recording during the 1920s – many with the Jean Goldkette and Paul Whiteman bands – before founding the Dorsey Brothers Orchestra in 1932. They feuded constantly, and split up in 1934 to form their own bands.

CARNEGIE HALL PROGRAM
Season 1937-1938
FIRE NOTICE—Look around *now* and choose the nearest exit to your seat. In case of fire walk (not run) to *that* Exit. Do not try to beat your neighbor to the street.
John J. McElligott, Fire Commissioner

CARNEGIE HALL
Sunday Evening, January 16th, at 8:30

S. HUROK
presents
(by arrangement with Music Corporation of America)

BENNY GOODMAN
and his
SWING ORCHESTRA

I.
"Don't Be That Way" — Edgar Sampson
"Sometimes I'm Happy" (from "Hit the Deck") — Irving Caesar & Vincent Youmans
"One O'clock Jump" — William (Count) Basie

II.
TWENTY YEARS OF JAZZ
"Sensation Rag" (as played c. 1917 by the Dixieland Jazz Band) — E. B. Edwards

PROGRAM CONTINUED ON SECOND PAGE FOLLOWING

improvization in his repertoire as he dared. The jazz numbers in his 'book' dominated the broadcasts that he made for the 'Camel Caravan' radio programme sponsored by the RJ Reynolds Tobacco Company. On the road, however, he felt he had to compromise. Arriving at the La Palomar Ballroom, Los Angeles, sometime in 1934, the band set out to please the dancers with 'sweet' material, but quickly realized that the applause was tepid. Disillusioned with public indifference and having intimations that his agent was having

trouble finding him work, he decided to throw caution to the winds and 'called' for the jazz numbers. To his astonishment the crowd reacted hysterically – they had wanted to hear 'live' what they had heard on the broadcasts. It was the beginning of an extraordinary upsurge in his fortunes, and provided a boost to the swing era generally. This popularity enabled Goodman to introduce a high incidence of improvization and to make numerous recordings with his trio, quartet and quintet that were wholly jazz, featuring black musicians, pianist Teddy Wilson, vibraphonist Lionel Hampton, and guitarist Charlie Christian.

The Goodman success inspired the

Top left: Goodman's fame could not be more clearly illustrated.

Top right: Carnegie Hall had previously presented only 'classical' music. This concert was to invest both Goodman and jazz in general with a hitherto unimagined degree of respectability.

Above: Goodman with Gene Krupa at the drums, and Teddy Wilson at the piano. Goodman was one of the first white band leaders to employ black musicians.

Far left: 'Stompin' at the Savoy' was one of Goodman's most popular numbers.

formation of many other bands in a similar mode, including those led by former Goodman sidemen – drummer Gene Krupa, and trumpeters Harry James and Bunny Berigan. Despite a hit recording with 'I Can't Get Started', Bunny Berigan's Band 'scuffled'. The leader, a brilliant musician with the most extensive range of all the white trumpeters, had a drink problem and in 1940, after going bankrupt, was compelled to rejoin a former boss, Tommy Dorsey. Not being in the position to give himself the solo space he had in his own band he became extremely frustrated. In June 1942 he was leading a band again but failed to make one of its engagements at New York's Manhattan Centre. Seriously ill with cirrhosis he died aged only 34, in June 1942. In contrast the Harry James Band, making a feature of James' bravura trumpet skills, was a highly successful undertaking, scoring million-selling hits with 'Ciribiribin' in 1939, 'You Made Me Love You' in 1941, and 'Easter Parade' in 1942.

Top left: Bunny Berigan, who left Goodman to form his own band, but failed, mainly due to personal problems. Ironically, his one hit was called 'I Can't Get Started'. He died of alcoholism at the age of 34.

Left: More establishment recognition for Goodman, seen here with 'classical' violinist Joseph Szigeti and Bela Bartok.

Above: Glenn Miller had been a colleague of Goodman's in the Ben Pollack Orchestra. He went on to lead what was probably the most successful swing band of all time.

Right: Woody Herman, another clarinettist/bandleader, styled his 1930s band unit 'The Band That Plays The Blues'.

Despite the intense competition, Benny Goodman remained the 'King of Swing', perhaps most strongly challenged by clarinettist Artie Shaw who aroused hysteria among his juvenile audiences, much to his own well publicized disgust. Frequently he dissolved his bands even though he was a top box office attraction, and the musical press were mystified that someone so successful should consistently turn his back on fame.

Throughout the 1930s a host of black bands were working continuously, although not attracting popular support at the same level as the crowds that Goodman, Shaw, the Dorseys and James were drawing. These included Fletcher Henderson, Andy Kirk (with pianiste Mary Lou Williams), Don Redman, Earl Hines, Cab Calloway, Louis Armstrong,

Above: Chick Webb, drummer and bandleader at the Savoy throughout the 1930s.

Right: Ella Fitzgerald, seen here aged sixteen, later became Chick's featured vocalist.

Above, far right: Members of Bob Crosby's Orchestra, 1936, with Joe Sullivan at the piano. The line-up is Irving Fazola, Gil Rodin, Bob Haggart, Nappy Lamare, Bob Crosby, Eddie Miller and Ray Bauduc. The Bobcat unit of which many of the above were a part, kept the small group tradition going through the 1930s.

Below, far right: Three white bandleaders of the period (left to right); Artie Shaw, Harry James, and Gene Krupa. Shaw was adored by his fans and was a contender for Goodman's crown as 'King of Swing'. However he was a temperamental individual, given to splenetic outbursts. He frequently went into these tantrums, during which he summarily fired his musicians. Harry James emerged from the 'school of' Benny Goodman to run his own band, which was very successful unlike that of his former colleague and fellow trumpeter, Bunny Berigan. Gene Krupa, the show-drummer supreme, is seen here in a very fine caricature by Boy ten Hove.

Swinging the Night Away

The Swing era lasted for approximately ten years. It was a time of widespread big band activity, both black and white, fuelled by the need for entertainment outlets during a period of economic depression (rather as, later, jazz was to enjoy an explosion of interest during the Second World War, as people sought ways to take their minds off the stresses of the conflict). Musically, especially in respect of the white bands, and

particularly from the purists' point of view, it was a time of varying quality, with the average performance contrasting uninspired arrangements of the often mediocre tunes churned out by Tin Pan Alley songsmiths with intermittent improvization of an unpredictable standard. However, when Swing was good it could be really good, and there were bands around at the time that produced some of the

finest and most exciting jazz music ever. These included white bands led by Jean Goldkette, Charlie Barnet, the Dorsey brothers (singly and collectively), Benny Goodman, Harry James, Artie Shaw, and Glenn Miller, and black bands under the leadership of Fletcher Henderson, Count Basie, Chick Webb, and, of course, Duke Ellington.

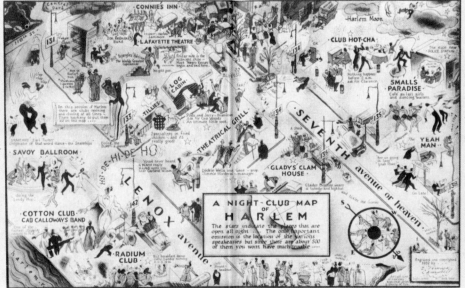

Understandably the art of swing dancing reached its height at venues like the Savoy Ballroom ('The Home of Happy Feet') in Harlem, where the almost wholly black clientele showed just how inventive and animated the steps could be. The great black orchestras that played the Savoy included its semi-resident band led by drummer Chick Webb and fronted at times by a fresh young vocal talent – Ella Fitzgerald.

Jitterbugs

Paradoxically the chief supporters of jazz music during the period were a section of the public that the critics had normally berated – the young 'jitterbugs', who cast aside the formal dancing conventions of their parents, and reacted to the music in an extrovert and animated manner. In fact, proper 'jitterbugging' was an art, requiring a sense of rhythm and a great deal of discipline to coordinate the steps between the partners.

Count Basie, Duke Ellington, and Chick Webb, the latter featuring the young Ella Fitzgerald. Her singing with the Webb Band on a novelty tune, 'A-Tisket, A-Tasket', became a million-seller during the 1930s. The Ellington Band was to reach one of its many peaks in the late 1930s when its rhythm section was transformed by the inclusion of a young bass player from Chattanooga, Tennessee – Jimmy Blanton. His exceptional prowess was demonstrated not only on the orchestra recordings but also on featured duets with Ellington.

Though the 1930s was the decade of the big band, some small groups continued working, mostly in the tiny clubs of 52nd Street, New York. A much recorded small band was the Bobcats from the large Bob Crosby Orchestra. With a nucleus of New Orleanians, they perpetuated the classic traditions in similar fashion to another New Orleanian, the one-armed trumpeter Wingy Manone. On his return to America after a five-year sojourn in Europe, the tenor saxophonist Coleman Hawkins formed a big band appearing at Kelly's Stables, 52nd Street. One of his features at Kelly's was a ten-chorus workout on the tune 'Body And Soul' which he recorded in 1939 for the Victor label. It sold a million. Although he used his full orchestra the record was essentially a Hawkins *tour de force* and its success is still one of the most astonishing events in the history of jazz.

Above left: A contemporary songsheet for a Duke Ellington composition.

Left: A Victor poster advertizing one of their biggest stars, 'Fats' Waller. Waller usually preferred to play with small units that set off his own talents, but he experimented with larger bands during the Swing era.

Above right: The Count Basie Band, 1941. Although Ellington could lay claim to the greatest number of star names, and the most sophisticated arrangements, when it came to sheer energy and excitement, nothing could beat Basie. He is seen here with one of his finest ensembles, including Lester Young on tenor saxophone (far right of the reed section); life-time Basie man Freddie Green on guitar (partially hidden); and Jo Jones on drums.

Right: The Apollo was one of the best jazz locations, continually featuring the finest black talent of the time. The consistently high standard is illustrated by this poster, advertizing, in a single three-week period, the appearance not only of the Basie band, but also of Andy Kirk and Jimmie Lunceford.

Far right: Pianist/bandleader Count Basie was born in New Jersey on 21st August 1904, and worked in the Kansas City area early in his career with Elmer Payne, and then Bennie Moten. Taking over the remains of Moten's group, he established his own band in 1934/5, later enlarging the ensemble and moving to New York. From then on he was to lead bands of different sizes, and with changing personnel, for nearly 50 years: he died in 1984.

Melody Maker

Vol. IX. No. 2 (New Series).   3 JUNE 1933   THREEPENCE.

SATCH'MO ARMSTRONG AGAIN

BACK FROM THE GRAVE TO THE HOLBORN

PREVIOUS HIT HOPED TO BE REPEATED

that is, form and rehearse one here. We hope that his experiences in this direction will not be beset by so many difficulties as they were last time.

At any rate, the forthcoming summer seems to hold bright prospects for dance music fans. ...stars has ...

Fred Elizalde to Challenge the Ether

The Melody Maker, 5 August 1933.

PIANO ACCORDIONS ?

Melody Maker

Vol. IX. No. 11 (New Series).   5 AUGUST 1933   THREEPENCE.

HOHNER only!
THE WORLD'S BEST
Write for Coloured Catalogue
HOHNER CONCESSIONAIRES
LIMITED
21 BEDFORD ST., STRAND, W.C.2

AMAZING RECEPTION FOR ARMSTRONG

FRENZIED APPLAUSE FOR MEANINGLESS PERFORMANCE

Louis Deliberately All Commercial

MAY FAIR PAIR TOPPING THE HOLBORN

DOUBLE PIANO SUPPORT

THE B.B.C. RATTLES THE SABRE

...OW OF THE STALLS!

... pianist ... since Co... trio he... rest a... be rem... piano ...

No fu... the Mill... is extre... tions which... are now in progress will be brought to a satisfactory conclusion, resulting in the appearance of the Four Boys and A Guitar in London.

And, finally, Louis. It is definite that he is booked for the Holborn Empire for July 31.

Louis is delighted at the prospect, and so, of course, are we, of renewing old friendships. We can promise him a royal time.

Dates

...okings after the Holborn are by ...settled, but the following have ...illed in":—Brighton Hippo... ...ust 7, and Birmingham ...ust 14. These dates ... ...later.

...he same procedure as he did last time.

Feathers Wafts Home

R. E. "BUDDY" FEATHERSTON-HAUGH, tenor sax stylist and Brooklands speed ace, is now leading his own trio at the new Bellometti's Restaurant in Soho Square.

"Buddy" plays hot tenor to rhythm supplied by Sam Costa, piano and vocal expert, and Stanley Marshall, percussion.

All three boys were members of the unit which Bert Firman took over to Monte Carlo during the winter season.

Bellometti's is a new and smart resort with a pint-sized dance floor.

...nner, we are sure that ...desire it, and we wish the very ...est of luck to one of the biggest triers in the game.

Jazz Consolidates in Britain

Louis Armstrong's arrival in Britain in July 1932 was a stepping stone for his first European tour: indeed, it was the first time he had ever played outside of the United States. He created a sensation, although much of the comment was unfavourable, even from enthusiasts who had revered his numerous recordings. They were unprepared for, and disapproved of, Armstrong the entertainer. As his initial appearance was at a variety theatre (the London Palladium), many reviewers in the lay press judged him by variety-hall standards, and found his singing 'uncouth' and his trumpet

Far left: *Melody Maker* front pages celebrate Armstrong's second coming, in 1933, but criticize his style and 'commercialism'.

Left: Armstrong accustomizing himself to the British way of life on his first, 1932, visit.

Below: A cartoon from *Melody Maker* in March 1931 takes a slightly patronizing line.

Louis Armstrong's First Lesson

"SURE, MAMMY – DE BOY'S GONNA BE A GREAT MAN WHEN HE'S DONE GROW'N UP!"

"CUT ALL DAT OUT, DAD! – I'SE GOIN' PLAY DE TRUMPET"

by Jorgen Myller

"IF YOU'SE MUST HAB A TRUMPET, LOUIS – WELL – YOU'SE MUST!"

MUSIC STORE

"DERE, LOUIS – DAT'S DE **LOWEST** NOTE ON DE TRUMPET!"

The Melody Maker, 17 June 1933.

Melody Maker

Vol. X. No. 4 (New Series).   17 JUNE 1933   THREEPENCE.

THE DUKE AT THE PALLADIUM

LONG AWAITED DEBUT TO PACKED HOUSES

JACK HYLTON STAGES A RECEPTION

by Our Special Representative

WELL! he's here! We have been reading about the Duke this last four or five years; he has become an almost legendary figure; it seemed impossible that we should ever see him in the flesh, or hear those amazing sounds other than via a gramophone. Yet, unbelievably, he is here.

A handful of us have been fortunate enough to be with, or not far from, the Duke ever since he docked in English waters. I am glad to say that I have been one of them; and I am very much aware that there are tens of thousands of Ellington fans round the country who would have given anything to come into such close contact with the Duke as I have been, so therefore, since it is hardly practicable for ten thousand people to follow Ellington wherever he goes, perhaps if I relate, in detail all that has happened, my readers may in some measure share my personal excitement and experiences.

Southampton.

The s.s. *Olympic* sailed from New York on Friday, June 2nd, it docked at Southampton at 12.30 Friday, June 9th. I was there with a crowd of others to welcome the Duke.

We went aboard the Olympic and sought him out. He was not difficult to find, for his light suit made him a conspicuous figure even from the quayside.

With Irving Mills we renewed our acquaintance of a few months ago. Irving, looking tanned and healthy, was wreathed in smiles, and wore a proprietary air of pride as he said "Meet the Duke!"

There he was! In person! In the flesh. The Duke! Himself!

Tall—over 6ft.—broad, with the shoulders, and build of an athlete, slightly plump in a way that seemed in accord with his obvious good temper.

A broad smile that had nothing artificial or forced about it. A firm handshake. A pleasant cultured voice.

Behind him were "the boys." There they were, all of them—Bigard, Hodges, Brown, Greer and the rest. Also in the party were two attractive coloured girls—Ivie Anderson, the blues singer, and Bessie Dudley, the dancer.

There was, of course, great to-do's. I think that the Duke's arm must have ached with the hundreds of handshakes! A constant procession of people passed in front of him: "Meet the Duke—this is Mr. So. and So!"

Poor Duke! All through all of it his smile never faltered and his good humour never cracked under the strain for an instant. The boys seemed a little overwhelmed.

Through the wizardry of Jack Hylton, the usually tedious Customs formalities

passed with lightning speed, and before very long Ellington was entrained, en route for London.

Waterloo.

At the London terminus the same scenes were repeated *ad libitum* and *fortissimo*. There were scores of familiar faces on the platform, and scores more of enthusiastic unknowns. The self-appointed reception committee looked like a Who's Who of the music industry. Everyone of any importance in it was there.

Once more the Duke and his boys underwent the ordeal of being lined up, photographed, hand-shaken, autographed-hunted, and asked absurd questions. They stood it very well.

Even when thirty-seven (I counted them!) photographers lined up and "shot" them, they remained pleasantly unperturbed.

The Hylton Reception.

Whilst the boys were settling down in their Bloomsbury Hotel, and taking their first look at London, the Duke was going through his third "ordeal" that day.

Jack Hylton has a beautiful house in Mayfair, which is typical of his independence of thought and disregard for convention. A strange place this of Jack's, from the outside. It looks like a Government building of some kind—long, low-roofed, and black-bricked lined with white. Inside, its appointments are luxurious. It cost a fortune, I believe, to convert this old building into the exquisite residence which it now is.

And at six o'clock that evening it was packed to overflowing. The front door stood permanently open, and a constant stream of people flowed in until it seemed that even this capacious place would hold no more.

There were representatives there from every paper that mattered. Hannen Swaffer, Tom Driberg ("William Hickey" of the *Express*), Garry Allighan, Gibson Young, Collie Knox, Cecil Hadley, and so on, and so on. Representatives of gramophone companies, distinguished "straight" musicians, and many others. All there to "Meet the Duke!"

Although all this was, of course, a terrific compliment, I really felt sorry for Ellington. If his handshaking at Southampton and Waterloo had been exhausting, then he really must have been prostrate that evening! Fortunately he has a physique that will stand it.

All the most ridiculous questions in the world were hurled at him. Even to

Duke Ellington greets England on his arrival on board the "Olympic"

the inevitable "What do you think of our policemen?"

But for everyone he had a pleasant smile, a ready answer and that wonderful and rare ability of making each single person to whom he spoke feel that that person was the most important in the room.

Broadcast.

The reception went on until shortly before nine o'clock. Then the Duke

was rushed off to Broadcasting House to say a few words into the mike.

I expect you all heard this, for it was put over at ten past nine, right in the middle of the news bulletin. Nothing was rehearsed, and Hylton and Ellington stood before the microphone and "made it up as they went along." Some people were unkind enough to say that it sounded like it, but surely it was better that way than a stilted and artificial reading of prepared notes!

The Duke's final remarks anent "being of little value without my band" are typical of his unassuming modesty.

The First Show.

As 6.30 p.m. approached on Monday, I must confess that my excitement rose to fever heat. Although Ellington's band was not on until nearly eight o'clock, I felt as though I shouldn't miss a bit of the whole bill at the Palladium. As a matter of fact I could have done so without serious loss, for, with the exception of Max Miller, the supporting acts were very poor. One supposes that the terrific cost of booking the band somewhat tied the hands of the bookers.

The house was packed from floor to roof, and there was not a seat to be had by the time the show opened. Yet, strangely enough, there were still seats for sale at a quarter past six. This was remarkable, and I can only imagine that it was because those who had not already booked thought they hadn't a chance of getting in. For once, fortune smiled on the improvident, and those who rolled up at the last minute "on spec." were surprised to find themselves in good seats.

It is unnecessary to say that the house was full of familiar faces, and everybody seemed to know everybody else.

The preceding acts went by all too slowly. Ellington was the last turn on the programme—No. 13. It seemed to me, when I discovered this, that it was bad placing, and the fact that the

playing 'shattering'. It was difficult for them to grasp the significance of someone the like of whom had never been seen before in Britain.

Despite this initially mixed reception, Armstrong made a tremendous impression, but his was essentially a solo triumph. The accompanying orchestras he 'fronted' were purely subsidiary to his playing, singing, and 'mugging'. The visit of Duke Ellington and his Orchestra in June 1933 was an entirely different matter. Here was a regular ensemble of unique talents and the public in general – not just the jazz enthusiasts – were overwhelmed by the spectacle of thirteen 'coloured' men performing magical flights of

Left: An excited welcome for Ellington.

Right: A poster advertizing one of the band's appearances.

Below: Duke Ellington and his Orchestra arrive at Southampton. Standing: Bessie Dudley, Bill Bailey, Sonny Greer, Fred Guy, Harry Carney, Otto Hardwicke, Barney Bigard, Spike Hughes (meeting them), Cootie Williams, Wellman Braud, Johnny Hodges, 'Tricky' Joe Nanton, Lawrence Brown, Ivie Anderson. Seated: Derby Wilson, Freddy Jenkins, Jack Hylton (impresario), Duke Ellington, Irving Mills (the manager), Juan Tizol, Arthur Whetsol.

ASTORIA DANCE SALON,

Charing Cross Road, W.C.2.

JACK HYLTON

holds a

MIDNIGHT BALL

and presents

DUKE ELLINGTON

AND

HIS FAMOUS ORCHESTRA.

From Midnight, Monday, June 19th, to 3 a.m., June 20th.

TICKETS 5/-

BOOK YOUR TABLES NOW.   Gerr. 1711.

improvization interwoven within a rich orchestral tapestry. It was a supremely imaginative and superbly executed distillation of Afro-American music – a revelation. Ellington was courted by intellectuals; by 'serious' music composers like Constant Lambert, Frederick Delius, and Percy Grainger; by members of the aristocracy, the press and even one of the royal family. Edward, Prince of Wales, heir to the throne, soon to be briefly King of England (then becoming Duke of Windsor after his abdication), was a keen follower of the band and 'sat in' on drums at a party held in honour of Ellington (with all his orchestra present) given by the press baron Lord Beaverbrook at his London mansion, Stornoway House, in Park Lane.

Following Ellington's sensational visit the British musicians' union raised objections to the further entry of American bands and put strong pressure on the Ministry of Labour to refuse them the essential work permits. Although the Ministry acquiesced, a few American bands and artistes did breach the ban. In March 1934 the 'King of Hi-De-Ho', Cab Calloway, and his Orchestra appeared at the Palladium, but suffered in comparison with Ellington's performances in the previous year. The reviewer in the *Melody Maker* was unenthusiastic. The most favourable comment he included was a compliment on 'the sartorial elegance of this band of coloured Beau Brummels'.

Groups that could be categorized as 'acts' *were* given permission to appear. These included the Washboard Serenaders in 1935; the Mills Brothers, who

made a speciality of instrumental imitations with their close harmony singing, in 1934, 1937 and 1939 (the latter a Royal Command Performance at the Palladium); and that rarity, a female jazz trumpeter, Valaida Snow, who appeared in Britain in 1935, 1936 and 1937. Singing and playing, she recorded with British musicians and mercilessly 'cut' the trumpeters on these sessions. In 1941, when touring Scandinavia, the German army invaded, and she was persecuted by the Gestapo.

Another jazzman booked as a variety 'single' was the irrepressible pianist/composer/singer Thomas 'Fats' Waller, who played the halls and recorded with British musicians, including trombonist George Chisholm. The latter recalls that an acolyte of Waller had only one function – to keep the fun man supplied with his favourite whisky, Haig: on one record Fats can be heard yelling for another bottle.

The performing prohibition was imposed on bands from other countries as well as America, but, again avoiding the ban by describing itself as a variety act, the Quintette du Hot Club of France with Europe's outstanding contribution to jazz, the gypsy guitarist Django Reindhardt, toured Britain in 1939.

Far left: The cover of the June 1935 issue of *Swing Music.*

Top: The vocalisms and histrionics of Cab Calloway, the showman band leader and 'King of Hi-De-Ho', upset the purists, but his band always included many good, albeit under-employed jazzmen. He was born in Rochester, New York, on 25th December 1907, and in the early years of his career worked as a singer and drummer in Baltimore and Chicago before fronting and leading a number of different bands in New York, including a spell at the Cotton Club. Even after the 1940s, when his bandleading success dried up, his popularity as a solo entertainer continued.

Above left: It is one of the great ironies of the history of jazz in Britain that Ellington's Orchestra, the greatest jazz ensemble ever, should cross the Atlantic to debut in a twenty-minute spot as a 'variety act', preceded on the bill by 'blue' comic Max Miller.

Left: An excellent caricature of the Duke.

Benny Carter

One exception to the rule applying to big bands was Teddy Hill and his Orchestra, who were allowed to take part in the Cotton Club Show at the Palladium in July 1937, provided that their participation was entirely musical and they did not 'move' except in the mechanics of playing their instruments. Although the band included several recognized jazzmen – including a then totally unknown trumpeter, Dizzy Gillespie – their rôle was purely to accompany the dancers and singers in the show.

Coleman Hawkins, regarded as the founding father of jazz tenor saxophone, was one genuine jazz musician to be granted a permit. Incongruously, he toured the variety halls with Mrs Jack Hylton's Band. He made a few recordings with British musicians before moving to Europe, playing in Switzerland and Holland and recording with the Dutch Ramblers Band. He was meant to tour Germany with Jack Hylton's Orchestra,

Left and below: The programme cover and running-order for the Swing Music Concert featuring multi-instrumentalist Benny Carter and his All-British Orchestra, held at the London Hippodrome and sponsored by *Melody Maker.*

The "Melody Maker" Concert of Swing Music

LONDON HIPPODROME, SUNDAY, JANUARY 10, 1937

FEATURING BENNY CARTER

PROGRAMME

1	"Swingin' at Maida Vale"	B. Carter
2	"Dream Lullaby"	B. Carter
3	"I Gotta Go"	B. Carter
4	"Chickfeed"	B. Carter

HARRY KARR
Saxophone Solos

5	"Believe It, Beloved"	T. Waller
6	"Big Ben Blues"	B. Carter
7	"These Foolish Things"	Strachey and Marvell
8	"When Day Is Done"	De Sylva and Katscher

HAROLD BEHRENS
"Odd Thoughts on Odder Subjects"

9	"Accent on Swing"	B. Carter
10	"Blue Interlude"	B. Carter
11	"Gin and Jive"	B. Carter

INTERVAL

12	"I'm in the Mood For Swing"	B. Carter
13	"Waltzing the Blues"	B. Carter
14	"When Lights Are Low"	B. Carter and S. Williams

BENNY CARTER
Melody Maker—Rhythm Accompaniment Records

15	"Symphony in Riffs"	B. Carter
16	"Nightfall"	B. Carter
17	"I Know That You Know"	A. Caldwell

JACK HYLTON'S "SWINGTETTE"

18	"Scandal in A Flat"	B. Carter
19	"Swingin' the Blues"	B. Carter

"JAM SESSION"

20	"Just a Mood"	B. Carter
21	"Nagasaki"	Dixon and Warren

GOD SAVE THE KING

Above: Another group to use the 'variety' loophole were the Mills Brothers, 'close harmony' singers who achieved instrumental impressions by glottal compression and cupping their hands over their mouths.

Above: 'Fats' Waller avoided the ban on visiting performers by appearing as a 'variety' act. He worked in Europe on many occasions during the 1930s, including trips to France, Germany and Denmark, as well as three separate visits to London. He died on 15th December 1943.

but was refused a visa because of his colour.

The flow of jazz recordings and the more frequent appearances of American bands and soloists were to have some effect on the repertoire and style of British dance bands, notably those of Lew Stone and Ambrose, and, to a lesser extent, Jack Hylton, Geraldo, Jack Harris, and Jack Payne. This was manifest in the occasional 'hot' number where the jazz-

Right: An EMI record celebrating the large number of black bands and performers who crossed the Atlantic during the 1920s and 1930s, and indicating the range of American talent that did tour during the period. The names include 'Fats' Waller, Duke Ellington and trumpeter Valaida, as well as lesser known acts such as Ike 'Yowse Suh' Hatch and his Harlem Stompers, Buck and Bubbles, and Noble Sissle and his Orchestra.

Right: A still from the film 'Pity The Poor Rich', which featured Nat Gonella and his Georgians. The Georgians toured the halls with an act highlighting Gonella's Louis Armstrong-inspired trumpet-playing and vocals. The band was not highly regarded by the critics, but it was popular with the public, and instrumental in attracting many people to the genuine jazz article. Compilations of Gonella's 78rpm records are still being issued over half a century later.

Far right: A rare early programme for the No. 1 Rhythm Club.

Below right: The committee of the No. 1 Rhythm Club, seen gathered around a gramophone, which may well have been a wind-up model. George Pennikett, Bill Elliott, Reg Southon, and an unknown man. Drummer Carlo Krahmer demonstrates his 'breaks' on period kit.

men in the ranks were given their head. Lew Stone's band recorded several instrumentals that exhibited the British players' partial grasp of the jazz idiom. However, it was no surprise that these were not always successful: the ban had deprived them of first-hand experience and they had to learn solely from gramophone records.

In Britain throughout the 1930s and 1940s there existed some two hundred rhythm clubs, numbered in the order of their founding, starting with the formation of the No. 1 Club in July 1933. The *Melody Maker* 'adopted' the movement and ran a column on its activities, which were mostly record recitals, but sometimes included jam sessions. The latter were a feature of the No. 1 meetings and on various occasions its distinguished visitors included Louis Armstrong, Benny Carter, Coleman Hawkins, and Garland Wilson. These rhythm clubs were to be the backbone of the jazz movement in Britain, acting as a pressure group on record companies and (much less successfully) on the BBC.

The Second World War saw the mushrooming of a myriad of clubs in London's West End, particularly in Soho. A thriving black market, the rise in prostitution to accommodate the many foreign and British servicemen, and the almost desperate need for recreational wartime diversions led to a marked increase in the

Top: Coleman Hawkins spent nearly five years in Holland (having been denied entry into Hitler's Germany because of his race) and did make some 78rpm recordings with the Dutch band The Ramblers, but the photograph on the album cover is misleading. In fact it shows Hawkins playing with members of Jack Hylton's Orchestra in London.

Above: A gathering of Britain's premier band leaders: Bill Harty, Phil Green, unknown man (perhaps a fan), Lew Stone, Christopher Stone (Britain's first Disc Jockey, although the term was not then in use), Carroll Gibbons, Harry Roy, Geraldo, Ray Noble, Henry Hall, Jack Hylton, Jack Jackson, Ambrose, and Howard Jacobs. The mystified lady is Mrs Christopher Stone.

popularity of improvized jazz. One famous, or infamous, spot was Jig's Club in St Annes Court, Wardour Street. The clientele was predominantly black and the resident band, led by trumpeter Cyril Blake with a fine guitarist, Lauderic Caton, played a rough and lively jazz that was entirely commensurate with the club's ambience. A frequent patron of Jig's (which, at one time changed its name to the Pool Club, probably after being closed down by the police) was the collector/writer/broadcaster Rex Harris. He was also a member of many other similar clubs, some of which had the briefest of lives, but all of which provided work for musicians with a yearning to play jazz rather than suffering the boredom of 'reading from the dots' in a conventional dance band (and for many who couldn't read music, anyway, but who could certainly improvize). The general upsurge in jazz appreciation during the war was to establish a seed-bed from which emerged a number of young musicians who, a few years later, were to give jazz a totally new dimension, playing what became known as bop, or rebop. Coincidentally, a school of amateur musicians, taking an entirely different route, and looking back to the past, was to effect a simultaneous revolution of its own – the 'Revival'.

Left: Jazz had a surge in popularity as people sought new ways to escape the stresses of the Second World War, which brought relative fame to previous unknowns such as Harry Parry.

Below left: Some of Rex Harris' membership cards (sometimes styled 'invitations' to avoid licensing regulations).

Above right: Popular drummer Freddie Crump shows his versatility. Among the onlookers are bandleader Johnny Claes (right of Crump, holding trumpet) and Ronnie Scott (whose head is just to the left of Claes), two of the musicians who were to have great influence in the shaping of the British jazz scene in the coming years.

Right: Service bands were a prominent wartime source of fresh jazz talent. The Blue Mariners scored a great hit at the 1942 Jazz Jamboree.

Far right: Victor Feldman received a tremendous amount of publicity as a child star, and carried on to become an important British jazz figure in later years.

("Daily Herald" photo)

OUR 7-YEAR-OLD KRUPA GOES TO TOWN!

This amazing action-picture of the "M.M." seven-year-old drum wizard, Victor Feldman, was taken at the No. 1 Rhythm Club on Sunday, when the child's incredible drumstics had a capacity audience by the ears.

At the conclusion of the show (reported on page one), Harry Parry announced that he is including Victor Feldman and his brothers in an early Radio Rhythm Club programme. He expressed his complete amazement at the child's capabilities—an opinion shared by all who have heard this young genius.

Jazz and the Establishment

After decades of being either ignored, misrepresented, or maligned, jazz began to assume a veneer of respectability after the Second World War, and suddenly public figures were happy to be seen and photographed with jazz musicians. In America successive presidents with, no doubt, an eye on the black vote, even entertained jazz men and women at the White House. President Kennedy's invitation to Nat King Cole and Jimmy Carter's to Charles Mingus are two such instances.

In Britain, one Prime Minister, Mrs Thatcher, has been photographed with jazzmen – though, again, as this was at a fund-raising event, the motivation may have been political rather than musical – and government ministers such as Kenneth Clarke freely admit that they like nothing better after a tiring late-night sitting of Parliament than to visit Ronnie Scott's for the second set. Jazz has even been blessed by contemporary royal approbation. Members of the royal family, including the current Prince of Wales, Prince Charles, have attended jazz concerts held in aid of charity.

Left: President Jimmy Carter puts a comforting arm around wheelchair-bound Mingus at an all-star jazz concert held at the White House on 18th June 1978. Mingus was overcome with emotion when the political guests and great musicians present honoured and applauded his contribution to jazz. Other jazzmen invited by Carter that day included Max Roach, Stan Getz, Ornette Coleman, Dexter Gordon, Dizzy Gillespie, Roy Eldridge and Lionel Hampton.

Above: President Kennedy with Nat King Cole at a White House reception. Sadly both were dead within a few short years of this photograph being taken: Kennedy, in 1963; and Cole on 15th February 1965. Cole was a brilliant jazz pianist: inspired himself by Earl Hines, Cole's work influenced a later generation including Horace Silver and Oscar Peterson.

Above: Mrs Thatcher could hardly be said to be looking relaxed, as she jams with British jazz notables Chris Barber, Dave Morgan and Kenny Ball. The meeting was recorded in the *Daily Mail*: 'Now here's a lady with soul in her iron . . . it's Tory leader Margaret Thatcher tentatively tootling on a clarinet in jazzy company at the House of Commons yesterday. The occasion was a warm-up for a concert at the Royal Albert Hall on October 25 to raise funds for the Fulham and Hammersmith North Conservative Associations. Starring with Mrs Thatcher were trombonists Chris Barber and Dave Morgan, and trumpeter Kenny Ball. Mrs Thatcher won't actually be playing at the concert. An aide revealed that she can't really play the clarinet at all. But, he added, 'she does like New Orleans jazz, especially Duke Ellington'.

Right: Prince Charles with John Barnes and Roy Williams at a charity gala.

Back to the Roots

Small bands appearing before the public were very much out of fashion by the mid-1920s, usually coming together only in the recording studios. The belief that bigger is better prevailed and once the swing craze of the 1930s had triumphed, the leading exponents, Jimmy Dorsey, Tommy Dorsey, Artie Shaw, and Benny Goodman, settled on a finely judged combination of 'killer-diller' arrangements for the jazz-minded fan and straight dance music with a leavening of vocals for the dancers.

Despite the overwhelming popularity of the swing units, the art of collective improvization had been perpetuated throughout the 1930s by Bob Crosby's Bobcats, which had emerged from the regular Crosby Orchestra, and in the little bands led by New Orleans trumpeters, Louis Prima and Wingy Manone. But few others maintained the earlier values, and there is no evidence of black bands playing in the New Orleans style at the time. It wasn't that New Orleans had become a jazz backwater – it was simply that the style with which the city was assumed to be associated had never really taken hold. New Orleans was vaguely recognized as the birthplace of those who had gone on to bigger things once they had moved

Left: 'The Revival' led to a renewal of interest in the great New Orleans jazzmen. Those still playing were to experience a tremendous resurgence in popularity, and were invited to make records such as 'New Orleans Jazz', recorded in 1940; and 'Kid Ory's Creole Jazz Band', recorded in 1954, which contains numbers first recorded by the band nearly thirty years previously.

Right: 'Jazzways', published in 1946, was one of the first serious jazz histories.

North, and the Hot Five and Hot Seven and Red Hot Peppers recordings, for instance, were regarded primarily as historical curios belonging to a vanished and barely documented era.

There seemed to be no reason why the big units shouldn't remain in the ascendancy. The leaders, after all, were exploiting a highly successful formula that reflected well in box office takings. Why should things change? But change they did, and ironically it was the emergence of the small bands playing traditional jazz that helped to seal the fate of the larger units.

These small bands were part of the phenomenon called 'The Revival'. It looked back to the roots of jazz, and in terms of its subsequent popular appeal it was an amazingly successful resurgence. 1939 was a key year in the saga: it saw the recordings of the white Muggsy Spanier Ragtime Band; the partnership between the white clarinettist and self-proclaimed dope peddlar, Milton 'Mezz' Mezzrow and the black New Orleans trumpeter Tommy Ladnier; Sidney Bechet's Feetwarmers; and 'Jelly Roll' Morton's return to a commercial studio, Bluebird, a subsidiary of the Victor organization with whom Morton had made his classic sides in the 1920s.

In 1940 four groups of musicians recorded for the Decca label in New York. The participants included trumpeters Louis Armstrong, Red Allen, and Natty Dominique; clarinettists Edmund Hall,

Above: Revivalism bred many small magazines that preached the gospel. This issue of *Jazz Writing* has Art Hodes (piano) and Mezz Mezzrow (clarinet), on the cover – two musicians who had emerged from the Chicago school and associated with Condon. Mezzrow was to profit greatly from the Revival, particularly in Europe, where he became a star attraction. Hodes, without neglecting his career as a performer, broadened his interests to become one of the most important chroniclers of the idiom, as editor of *Jazz Record*, and as a writer, lecturer, and TV broadcaster. Other articles in this issue of *Jazz Writing* look back to 'Negro' music of the 1890s, New Orleans at the turn of the century, 'Jelly Roll' Morton, and the Louisiana Five.

Top: Kid Ory features on another traditional journal, *Pickup*, in 1947.

Above: Aptly named 'The Great 16', this compilation of sixteen 78rpm sides by Muggsy Spanier's Ragtime Band is, 50 years later, regarded as a supreme example of solo and collective improvization in the classic style. Spanier was born in Chicago on 9th November 1906. A cornet player, heavily influenced by the early work of Armstrong and King Oliver, he played with Ted Lewis and Ben Pollack before forming the Ragtime Band in 1939.

BUNK JOHNSON
AND HIS NEW ORLEANS BAND

FEATURING

GEORGE LEWIS   BABY DODDS

JIM ROBINSON   SLOW DRAG

LAWRENCE MARRERO   ALTON PURNELL

DANCING

TUESDAY, WEDNESDAY, THURSDAY and **FRIDAY NIGHTS**
From 8:30 P. M. to 12:30 A. M.

and **SUNDAY AFTERNOONS** from 2:00 to 5:00 P. M.

STUYVESANT CASINO

140 SECOND AVENUE   Near 9th Street   NEW YORK CITY

Two Blocks East of Wanamaker's

Easily reached by all main subway, "L" and bus lines. From West Side Lines, take 8th Street crosstown bus to Second Avenue.

ADMISSION: $1.00, Incl. Tax   Sundays, 80c, Incl. Tax

Sidney Bechet, Johnny Dodds and Jimmy Noone; and the trombonist Preston Jackson: all these came from New Orleans, and the 78rpm recordings were issued as the 'New Orleans Album'. All the musicians involved had recorded previously, but it was soon the turn of others to occupy the stage. These were a coterie of New Orleans musicians who had never left their home town, had never made gramophone records, and only a very few of whom had previously received any mention in jazz literature.

The first of these recordings was made in New Orleans in 1940, by trumpeter Kid Rena's band. Rena had worked regularly in the city and surrounding districts throughout the 1920s and 1930s, and his street band included a part-time musician – a longshoreman by day – clarinettist George Lewis. Later, in 1942, Lewis was in a band led by trumpeter Bunk Johnson that, in a room above a record shop in New Orleans, commenced a lengthy series

One Veteran is Last Link With Buddy Bolden

Dave Stuart Stages Unique Session in New Orleans

Los Angeles—Dave Stuart, who set the jazz world on its ear by releasing an album by the Yerba Buena Jazz Band (with its two banjos), has just returned from New Orleans with the masters for what will probably be the most historically important jazz records made since the late Jelly Roll Morton was recorded by General Records for the Library of Congress.

All More Than 50

Stuart's latest venture consists of a series of records he caught down in New Orleans after rounding up a band of old time jazz men—all over 50 years of age—and topping them off with Bunk Johnson, 62-year-old Negro cornet player who is the last important connecting link between the present and the fabulous Buddy Bolden, whose band Johnson joined in 1895.

The discs made by the group of old-time New Orleans jazz men were devoted to the old standards that formed the basis for jazz—*Moose March, Panama, Ballin' the Jack, Down By the River, Bunk's Blues, Storeyville Blues, Weary Blues, Oh, Lord I'm Crippled,* and *Make Me a Pallet on the Floor.*

Tells Jazz Story

Set is topped off with three sides of monologue by Johnson in which the old timer tells stories of the early days of jazz in his own words.

Johnson and the others had played little in the past 10 years if at all, but rusty as their technique is, the authenticity of their music is unquestioned. Complete personnel consists of Johnson, cornet; George Lewis, clarinet; Jim Robinson, trombone; Walter Decou, piano; Austin Young, bass; Ernest Rogers, drums; Tony Morraro, banjo.

Les Brown Triple Lo Armed F

Los Angeles — three more boys to ices during his st wood Palladium. A Shelley Manne, dr the fourth hide po ate directly from into the service of

A tough one to Mose, the clarine been one of the Brown's band. He army band at the S ing camp near he one-time Goodman

LOS A

By HAL HOLLY

Los Angeles— his band into to If the Troeader cretion we'd say for F.B.I. candie the identity of the attraction draws t voice that carries mediate violence) : know?" Well, you fellow. After all, ity would prompt what goes on at What difference Certainly none to

However, as far able to determine return there with July 9, and Phil ranger (currently for Bob Crosby) to ranging special nu Horne to sing at t that he also directs from the piano du tations there. Now bo wants to sue this information 648 N. Rampart geles. Any publici gains from this a purely accidental

Left: The cover of the *Jazz Record* of November 1945. The caption to this shot reads: 'Willie "Bunk" Johnson – Born December 27, 1879, in New Orleans. Started playing cornet at the age of 10, and in 1894, at the age of 14, graduated from music school. In that year he joined Adam Olivier's band, and then went with Buddy Bolden. Credited with being Louis Armstrong's teacher and inspiration, Bunk had been out of music for many years until his recent come-back in San Francisco and his present New York engagement. He has recorded for Jazz Man and A.M. labels, and will do more recording before the New York engagement ends.'

Above: A contemporary music newspaper cutting showing the interest in Revivalism.

Far left: One legendary figure particularly revered by Revivalists was Bunk Johnson. This poster advertizes his first performance in New York in 1945.

of recordings. It was seen by the musical press as an exercise in nostalgia, the aim merely to enshrine on wax some ancients associated with the origins of jazz. But the repercussions were astonishing. Within a few years literally hundreds of young whites (but not a single black) were emulating the Bunk Johnson band, with the clarinettists, particularly, copying George Lewis, making him the most imitated of all jazz clarinettists, with the exception of Benny Goodman.

Many, many musicians who had left the business, or were working only part-time, now enjoyed a new lease of life, including trumpeter Mutt Carey, who had been a Pullman porter; trombonist Kid Ory, who had been running a chicken farm; and clarinettist Albert Nicholas, who had been working as a New York subway guard. In San Francisco, a dance band trumpeter, Lu Watters, formed a white band that played principally in the style of King Oliver's Creole Jazz Band – not as a gimmick, but in genuine obeisance to the pioneers. The fact that they were far behind their New Orleans mentors in inspiration and technique wasn't noticed by the enthusiastic crowds attending the Dawn Club where the band was resident, and the partisan critics, in their keenness to laud the band's

Bottom and below: Lu Watters and his Yerba Buena Jazz Band and a poster advertizing their appearance at the Dawn Club. The line-up here features key band members Turk Murphy, Watters, and Bob Scobey. Lu 'Luscious' Watters was born in Santa Cruz on 19th December 1911. He played in various West Coast groups before

founding the Yerba Buena unit in 1939 specifically to perform old-style jazz music: they are often described as the first Revivalist ensemble.

Right: Mutt Carey, whose career as a Pullman porter was cut short by fame during the Revival.

record *changer*

jazz records section
. . . . . **page 11**

classical records section
. . . . . **page 48**

25¢
nov. '46

Mutt Carey

Above: Louis Armstrong, Billie Holiday, and Barney Bigard on the set of the film 'New Orleans' in 1946. Barney (Albany Leon) Bigard was born in New Orleans on 3rd March 1906. He was a highly creative and imaginative clarinettist who contributed an important element of New Orleans style and quality to Ellington's band in the 1920s and 1930s. After Bigard had worked with Armstrong in 'New Orleans', Louis invited him to join the All-Stars, with whom he worked for five years. The film 'New Orleans' was universally condemned by the jazz fraternity as a waste of talent and a misrepresentation of the true origins of the idiom.

Right: The Condon mob still going strong in the 1940s, seen here playing a 'Town Hall Concert' during a visit to Britain. Condon is on guitar, with Tony Parenti on clarinet, and 'Wild Bill' Davison.

Far right: Davison was a survivor, despite a rough and rugged lifestyle in which alcohol featured liberally. Born in Ohio on 5th January 1906, his early career was not spectacular, and was nearly cut short by a lip injury he received during a bar room altercation. He established a reputation with Condon in the 1940s, and went from strength to strength as a recording artist and soloist for the next 40 years. He died in 1990.

aims, overlooked their deficiencies.

The revival saw other white musicians riding the wave, particularly the group known as the 'Condon mob' under the direction of guitarist Eddie Condon. Out of these emerged the trumpeter Wild Bill Davison, who had been totally unknown before the early 1940s. Some of the heavy drinking alumni, such as trombonist Lou McGarity, Miff Mole and Cutty Cutshall, were more than happy to leave the big

bands in which they had previously earned their living, mostly by 'reading the dots'. The changed situation led to a spate of reissues on a multiplicity of labels, of recordings by early bands and blues singers. And not only by New Orleans, or New Orleans-style bands, but also early recordings by the likes of Fletcher Henderson and Duke Ellington, much to the embarrassment of these leaders and their surviving sidemen. In truth, it is hard to

believe that Ellington's band of the 1940s had any genuine connection with his somewhat crude efforts of the early 1920s.

These discoveries were enthusiastically reviewed in the little home-produced magazines which had, for the most part, attacked the commercial values that had enabled a monster as corrupt, mechanical, slick, and insincere as swing music to swamp the original, genuine article. Conversely the more established magazines,

such as *Esquire*, savaged what they saw as a retrogressive move and a reactionary denial of progress.

Revivalism spread throughout the world. Those significant recordings of the early 1940s were largely responsible for the cult of New Orleans jazz that took grip in Britain. In 1942 in a dull suburb of South London, Barnhurst, the Bexleyheath and District Rhythm Club, number 130 in the *Melody Maker* listing of clubs,

Left: George Webb, born in London on 8th October 1917, was the most important figure in the post-war British jazz Revival. His Dixielanders were a regular attraction on the London jazz circuit of the 1940s.

Below: George Webb's Dixielanders, caricatured by the band's clarinettist, the renowned cartoonist Wally Fawkes.

was born. Meeting on Monday evenings, their normal pattern was a record recital by a collector followed by a jam session. The tenor saxophone – Coleman Hawkins was the usual mentor – was the predominant instrument, accompanied by a rhythm section of piano, bass, drums and guitar. The club was infiltrated by musicians with revivalist aims, notably cornettist Owen Bryce and pianist George Webb. Soon they had recruited like-minded players to form George Webb's Dixielanders, with the traditional instrumentation of trumpet, trombone, clarinet, and a rhythm team that employed the tuba and banjo instead of string bass and guitar.

Technically limited, the Dixielanders were to become the seminal New Orleans-style band in Britain, their rough honesty and patent sincerity impressing club members and creating a weekly pilgrimage

Cartoon by Wally Fawkes

GEORGE WEBB'S DIXIELANDERS

Left: The Marquis of Donegal compereing at the last concert of the Hot Club of London in January 1948. The Marquis, a great supporter of, and servant to, jazz, had been responsible for the appearance of the Original Dixieland Jazz Band before King George V and Queen Mary at Buckingham Palace in 1919.

Right: A Hot Club poster advertizing an appearance of George Webb's Dixielanders.

Below: Humphrey Lyttelton and his Band, with George Webb on piano. Lyttelton was born on 23rd May 1921. Having played with George Webb's Dixielanders in the 1940s, and having created a reputation for himself as an exceptional trumpet prospect, Lyttelton took over the remains of the band in 1948, and established it as the foremost Revivalist group in Britain. They made some fine recordings in the early 1950s.

HOT CLUB OF LONDON

Recitalist

Owen Bryce

GEORGE WEBB'S
Dixielanders

Christie Bros. . Stompers

Ray Foxley

Rag Pianist

KING GEORGE'S HALL
ADELINE PLACE, GT. RUSSELL STREET, W.C.1.
(Near Tottenham Court Road Tube)

SATURDAY, JULY 5th
7.30—10.30 p.m.   DOORS OPEN 6.30 p.m.
Admission 3/6   Members 2/6
Tickets from—Hot Club of London, 23 Thomas Street
London, S.E. 18. WOO. 3631 (between 9-6 only) or at door.

SEND S.A.E. WITH REMITTANCE

Arcan Press, 73 Garland Road, S.E. 18

by enthusiasts from well outside the area. In April 1947 they were joined by trumpeter Humphrey Lyttelton, straight from the Brigade of Guards where he had held the rank of captain. He left to form his own band in December that year: his social background gained him considerable publicity, but he was an outstanding player in his own right. His band quickly became highly successful and he has been a band leader continuously ever since.

In November 1949 the glad tidings, spread by the jazz bush telegraph, was that Sidney Bechet was to play, unofficially, a concert in London. The promoters, Bert and Stan Wilcox were presenting a concert featuring Humphrey Lyttelton and his Band at the Winter Gardens Theatre, Covent Garden, and on the night of the concert, 13th November, Bechet was seated in the Royal Box and 'invited' by compere Rex Harris to 'sit in' with the band. Bechet accepted the 'invitation' and walked on to the stage to a tumultuous reception. Such was the overwhelming joy that the roar of the audience drowned the first few bars: here, at last, was a giant of jazz playing before their very eyes. Inevitably there were legal repercussions, and the Wilcox brothers were heavily fined. But the event had proved, beyond doubt, the enormously strong feeling that

Left: Lyttelton, inset during his schooldays at Eton (he is on the left), reversed the normal state of affairs in the 1950s by having his British jazz recordings released in America.

Top and above: Bechet, on his visit to Britain following an appearance at the Paris Jazz Festival, goes on stage at the Winter Garden to break the Musician's Union ban at the invitation of the Wilcox brothers.

Right: George Melly, one of the key figures in British jazz history. He was born in Liverpool on 17th August 1926, and began his singing career on tour with the Mick Mulligan band during the 1950s, after which he fronted various combinations with a mixture of classic jazz songs and modern, often bawdy, material. He also wrote some of the best ever books on jazz and the life of a jazz musician, including 'Owning Up' and 'Revolt Into Style'. His wit and eloquence have brought him great popularity as a broadcaster, presenter and critic on a wide range of subjects.

Below: The Crane River Jazz Band from Cranford in Middlesex were the first British band to attempt to emulate the Bunk Johnson–George Lewis style.

musicians of the calibre of Bechet should have been allowed to play in Britain. It was to be several years before such arrangements were officially made, and then not without persistent pressure on the authorities by a vocal fraternity.

Another veteran, Coleman Hawkins, appeared – also illegally – at the Princess Theatre, Cambridge Circus in December 1949, and the promoters involved were also fined. The Hawkins concert was not as ecstatically received as Bechet's, the principal reason being that in the mid-1940s jazz had split into two mutually antagonistic camps: traditionalism and modernism. The latter movement emerged in America, almost simultaneously with revivalism, and there it was called bop or rebop. Hawkins, while highly revered for the recordings he made with Fletcher Henderson in the 1920s and 1930s, had been playing with the boppers. On the occasion of the Princess Theatre concert, section was in the modern his rhythm idiom, and although the audience comprised both modernists and traditionalists, the differences of opinion and reaction reflected the schism that was to divide the jazz world for many years. It was indeed ironic that two entirely different and quite unexpected forms of jazz combined to see the end of big bands.

Above: Graeme Bell's Australian Jazz
Band, c.1945. The 'Bells' were the first and
only Australian jazz band to tour Europe,
commencing a residency in Prague in 1947
They brought with them an unpretentious
style that helped to lighten attitudes to jazz,
which had a tendency towards over-
seriousness at the time.

Right: Louis Armstrong on his 1949 visit to
London, with Max Jones. Jones has an
important part in British jazz history as one
of its most knowledgeable and highly
regarded commentators, critics and
archivists. He edited the 'Collectors's
Corner' section of the *Melody Maker,* and
wrote the excellent biography of Louis
Armstrong, 'Louis', with John Chilton
(Studio Vista, 1971).

The Bebop Revolution

When the challenge to the old order called bebop first appeared, no one, particularly its practitioners, would have given any credence to the thought that it was a commercial proposition. It was simply too revolutionary; seemingly dissonant, and often played at a breakneck speed unsuitable for dancing.

Bebop evolved almost clandestinely, in very few locations. The exponents were all black, and there was a racial dimension to the experimentation. The black musicians had long been aware that their phrases – their 'licks' and 'riffs' – and their compositions had been lifted by white musicians, and they had seen these inferior white bands becoming commercially successful. One aim of bebop was to create a music that the white man could not steal. Although the racial origins of jazz have never been fully determined, that bebop was a black innovation is indisputable.

The most significant characteristic of this new jazz was the highly diversified texture created by the rhythm section, in contrast to the insistent four-beats-to-the-bar common in the swing bands. In bebop the basic beat was stated by the bassist and elaborated on the cymbal and high hat by the drummer, with chordal punctuations, rather than by the old-style 'um-ching' from the pianist. The four-to-a-bar role of the guitarist had no place in the bop rhythm section and was discarded. The greater rhythmic options spurred the soloist to daring flights of improvization.

The genesis of bop was in a dilapidated dining room in the Hotel Cecil, West 118th Street in the Harlem district of New York. A former saxophone player, Henry Minton, took over the premises and called it Minton's Playhouse. It was later managed

Left and above: Album covers for recordings by Charlie 'Bird' Parker. Charlie Parker was born in Kansas City on 29th August 1920, and died in New York on 12th March 1955. One of the legendary figures, Parker has, more than any other musician, become an icon of the world of jazz. He learnt the saxophone at school, and left at fourteen to devote all his time to perfecting his technique. His early hero was Kansas-based Lester Young, and he was later to work with him and all of the great contemporary names, including Dizzy Gillespie, Ben Webster, Earl Hines, and Miles Davis, becoming the single most influential musician in the creation of Bop. His lifestyle included periods of alcoholism and drug addiction, but his musicanship was unrivalled, and with the possible exception of Armstrong, his influence on the idiom is unequalled.

Left and below left: Dizzy Gillespie, and a cutting from *Down Beat* charting his ups and downs as a band leader. Another significant figure, in collaboration with Parker, in the development of the new jazz idiom of Bebop, like Parker, Gillespie's reputation transceded identification with a single style, and he, too, is one of the truly great jazzmen. Born in South Carolina on 21st October 1917, he worked with Cab Calloway and Billy Eckstine before forming his own band in the 1940s.

by another saxophonist, Teddy Hill, known principally for his tenure with the roaring Luis Russell Band at its peak in the late 1920s. On Monday evenings a clique of musicians met for jam sessions, which most definitely were not the usual run of the mill 'blows'. Although the hard core of the group (pianists Thelonious Monk and Bud Powell, trumpeters Dizzy Gillespie and Joe Guy, drummer Kenny Clarke, and alto saxophonist Charlie Parker) experimented with the new patterns mostly for their own satisfaction, the new music caught on, attracting many other young musicians who were equally tired of the well worn harmonic paths. Bebop moved into 52nd Street, the 'Street That Never Sleeps', to attract a curious public and to receive the attention of the musical press. It was not long before it was being played in the concert halls.

In 1945 Gillespie formed his own big band, but the time was not right for so many musicians, some fifteen pieces, playing a style that was still a startling departure from the norm. For the next five years he alternated between big and small units before finally abandoning the big band format, except for specific projects. Like his fellow innovator, Charlie Parker, Gillespie earned considerably more money as an occasional sideman in Granz's Jazz at the Philharmonic, a concept of jazz that – despite being attacked for its sensationalism and vulgarity – continued throughout the 1960s to be highly

Right: Theolonius Monk was born in North Carolina on 11th October 1917, and spent his early years in New York, studying at one time at the Juilliard School. With Parker and Gillespie, he was part of the Minton set when Bebop was taking shape and played a full part in its conception. He had his own groups in the 1950s and 1960s, including members such as Art Blakey and John Coltrane, until ill health forced him to retire in 1974. He died in 1982.

popular with the public, who largely ignored the purism of the critics.

Out of the basic bop style evolved what was known as cool jazz, of which many of the foremost practitioners were white musicians. Their aim was to remove themselves even further from the old-fashioned 'heat' and to play in a detached manner in which understatement was the essence. Ironically, the principal rôle model was a pre-war musician, tenor saxophonist Lester Young, whose history stretched

Above: 'Cool jazz' was the first refinement of bebop, and its king was Miles Davis. Bop, as personified by Parker, had two distinct sides: one aggressive and stormy; the other more tranquil and reflective. Having experienced both in his years with Gillespie and Parker, Davis was interested in the possibilities of developing the contemplative elements within a larger framework rather than in the small units ideally suited to bop. The result was a series of recordings made on 78rpm between January 1949 and March 1950,

featuring among many others, musicians Gerry Mulligan, and Lee Konitz, and the organization of arrangers Gil Evans and John Lewis. These recordings were subsequently issued in pairs, and in 1957 were collectively released on a single compilation: 'The Birth Of The Cool'. The group never gelled as a 'live' band, and Davis worked with other small units in the 1950s before forming a quintet which included John Coltrane. With Gil Evans again arranging, they produced some exceptional recordings.

back to King Oliver's 1930 band, and whose solos – so unlike his principal rival, Coleman Hawkins – graced so many Count Basie recordings in the 1930s. The musicians involved in cool jazz included saxophonists Stan Getz, Lee Konitz, Art Pepper and Gerry Mulligan; trumpeters Miles Davis and Chet Baker; pianists Lenny Tristano and Dave Brubeck; and the Modern Jazz Quartet. The 78rpm recordings that Miles Davis made were later issued in album form as 'The Birth Of The Cool'. Other musicians involved in this development were the expatriate British blind pianist George Shearing with his quintet, and the arranger Gil Evans,

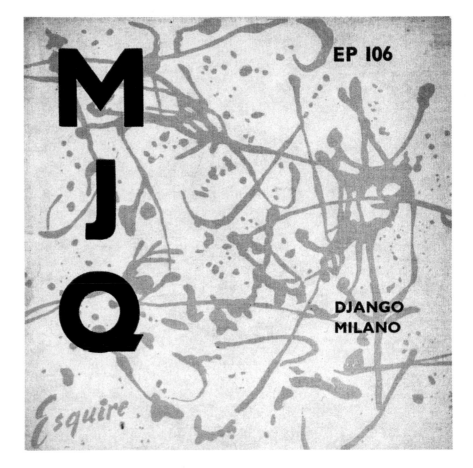

Right: Formed from fringe members of the Minton set, the Modern Jazz Quartet was founded in 1952, originally under the name of the Milt Jackson Quartet. It first appeared under the revised title in 1954, at which time the personnel were John Lewis, piano (and musical director); Milt Jackson, vibes; Percy Heath, bass (who had replaced previous Milt Jackson member Ray Brown); and Kenny Clarke, drums.

Above: Trumpeter/vocalist Chet Baker.

Left: Lester Young was born in Mississippi on 27th August 1909. His contribution to jazz in general, and to the language of the tenor saxophone in particular, was immense, and every saxophone player of his own and succeeding generations (with the exception of his great rival Coleman Hawkins) has been heavily influenced by his ideas.

who conceived the innovative orchestrations which were a backcloth to Miles Davis' ethereal improvizations on such classic recordings as 'Porgy and Bess' and 'Sketches of Spain'. Inevitably, many musicians combined elements of basic bop and its 'cool' offshoot. Jazz was becoming increasingly multi-faceted.

The bop phraseology permeated the big bands such as Woody Herman, Stan Kenton and Boyd Raeburn. Others, like Tommy Dorsey and Benny Goodman, criticized the new jazz heavily, their objections probably based on honest criticism, although they must have also seen it as a threat to their long-standing popularity.

Right: Woody Herman carried on leading big bands throughout the 1940s and 1950s. His acknowledgement of the radical changes in jazz going on around him was to employ fresh young talent, such as Stan Getz and Zoot Sims, and to allow his soloists to express themselves in the mood of the times.

Below: Miles Davis working with Gil Evans in 1957, at around the time his quintet was recording 'Miles Ahead', 'Sketches from Spain', and 'Porgy and Bess'.

Above: Sarah Vaughan, one of the great vocalists to embrace the jazz idiom, worked with Billy Eckstine in his big bop band, having previously spent some years with Earl Hines. Born in New Jersey on 27th March 1924, she had a tremendous popular following throughout a long and distinguished career.

The first big bop band was led by singer Billy Eckstine, its personnel at various times including trumpeters Dizzy Gillespie and Miles Davis, and saxophonists Charlie Parker and Dexter Gordon. Well in advance of its time, it was a short-lived venture despite concessions to ballroom dancers. It featured an outstanding female singer, Sarah Vaughan, who was soon to acquire the cognomen of the 'Divine Sarah'.

Aside from all these developments in jazz there was yet another entity that had a definite character of its own: this was the series of 'Jazz at the Philharmonic' concerts organized by a shrewd entrepreneur, Norman Granz. In the polariz-

Above and right: Pianist band leader Stan Kenton, seen above advertizing haircream and toothpaste in a single photograph, was born in Kansas on 19th February 1912, and played with various bands on the West Coast, before founding his own group in 1940. It was essentially a dance and swing band, but Kenton had a leaning towards modernism which grew through the decade until it resulted, in the early 1950s, in the formation of a band consisting of over 40 musicians, which he called The Innovations in Modern Music Orchestra. It flopped (perhaps predictably) and Kenton quickly returned to his commercially successful swing formula.

ation of traditionalists versus modernists, Granz recruited musicians of neither specific persuasion for his packages, the main constituent of which was rabble-rousing excitement. The trumpeters were constantly reaching for the high notes, the saxophonists honked and swayed, and the drummers took lengthy solos. The title stemmed from one of Granz's earlier promotions staged at the Los Angeles Philharmonic Auditorium. Ironically, the management of the Auditorium later barred his presentations as being 'unsuitable'. The Jazz at the Philharmonic was immensely popular with the larger public and made Granz a fortune, out of which he paid his musicians well. They, with such generous remuneration, could overlook the criticisms of the purists who

attacked the Jazz at the Philharmonic on all fronts as vulgar and sensationalistic. The stars that Granz used were trumpeters Roy Eldridge and Howard McGhee; trombonists JJ Johnson and Bill Harris; tenor saxophonists Coleman Hawkins, Flip Phillips, Stan Getz and Don Byas; alto saxophonists Benny Carter and Willie Smith; drummers Gene Krupa, Buddy Rich and JC Heard; and a brilliant young pianist from Montreal, Oscar Peterson. As mentioned, bebop stars Dizzy Gillespie and Charlie Parker were also included in these presentations.

From its beginning, bop, and its subsequent manifestations, was savagely attacked by the fundamentalists, and the traditionalist-modernist conflict raged. The traditionalists alleged that the 'screwy'

Above: Norman Granz's Jazz At The Philharmonic extravaganzas were a unique jazz phenomenon. Taking neither side in the modernist/traditionalist argument, they were pure entertainment, taking some of the finest and most explosive talent of the day and setting it in an environment which encouraged the musicians to express themselves in the most exciting possible way. Though scorned by purists (of both camps) as vulgar and commercial, they were highly successful with the paying public, and a spell with Jazz At The Philharmonic could prove very lucrative for any performer. The concerts started in 1944, originally as a one-off benefit for victims of racial riots in Los Angeles, and continued until 1957, with a brief revival in 1967.

Left and right: Programmes for Jazz At The Philharmonic concerts in the United States and on tour in Britain.

Above: Pianist Art (Arthur) Tatum was born in Ohio on 13th October 1909. Though almost blind he performed continuously until his death in 1956.

"THE CAT"

"Here y'are, bud! Get your biography of Wham Rebopp, I wrote it myself; don't miss his latest platter, an original by me; here's the new issue of Monotone Magazine, in which I review the record; have you read my new book on jazz; you'll surely want my latest photograph of the band; and oh yes—here's a couple of passes—on me!"

Above: Gene Deitch created the most potent anti-traditionalist symbol of all in Braywood Leather, his caricature of the English bebop enthusiast and defender Leonard Feather.

effects were a denial of the music's essence, and pointed specifically to the sartorial idiosyncrasies of Dizzy Gillespie, with his dark glasses, beret, 'zoot' suits and goatee beard. He was seen as the grimacing Grimaldi of the new jazz and condemned accordingly. The objections were particularly heated in the magazine *Jazz Record* edited by pianist Art Hodes and his Greenwich Village printer Dale Curran, and in the *Record Changer*. In one issue of the latter, cartoonist Gene Deitch created a meaningful caricature of a manifestly 'smart operator' who was a composer, pianist, session organizer and journalist called Braywood Leather. Obviously, it was lampooning the expatriate British apologist for bebop, Leonard Feather, who had become the main butt of the traditionalists. Feather's retaliation came via his columns in the glossy *Esquire* and *Metronome* magazines, where he nicknamed his adversaries 'Mouldy Fygges'. He and other modernists scornfully pointed to their retrogressive attitudes

Left: *Record Changer* was a very influential magazine in the 1940s and 1950s, taking the traditionalist line against the new jazz. In the 1940s it was published in Washington, and Gordon Gullickson was owner as well as Editor-Publisher, but it moved to La Salle Street, New York in the 1950s, under a new Editor-Publisher, Bill Grauer (listed in the staff of 1946 as Commercial Advertizing manager).

THE CAT

"Now let me get this deal straight: you say you can get me every record I ever asked for. . . . Surely you must want *something* from me!?!"

and to the poor musicianship of many of the old-timers who had been resuscitated. Deitch was not in fact completely unaware of the foibles and idiosyncrasies of his fellow 'Fygges': his main character, 'The Cat', was a quintessential 'Mouldy Fygge', overly concerned with the superficialities – labels, matrix numbers, romantic illusions and irrational partisanship – rather than with jazz music itself.

The controversy and consequent polarization of traditional and modern jazz was to divide enthusiasts throughout all parts of the world where it was played and heard, and this was particularly so in Britain. Unlike traditional jazz, that now had representative bands throughout the country, British bop was initially a specifically metropolitan phenomenon, and as secluded and conspiratorial as the Minton sessions. The young British tyros were handicapped by two factors: one was the scarcity of the records they could study; the other was the continuing ban on all American musicians, depriving the local players of the opportunity to hear the

Above: Johnny Dankworth with the members of his band The Johnny Dankworth Seven, which was among the foremost of the new British bop groups. Dankworth is centre, then (clockwise from the top) Don Rendell, Jimmie Deuchar, Tony Kinsey, Eric Dawson, Bill Le Sage, and Eddie Harvey. Dankworth was born on 20th September 1927, and studied at the Royal Academy of Music, while playing the clarinet in traditional bands in the evenings. Becoming interested in bop, he signed on with 'Geraldo's Navy' to experience it first hand.

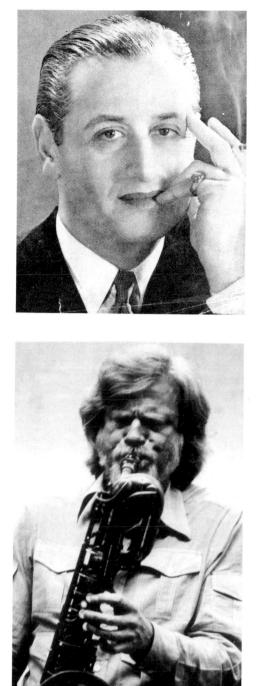

Top: The urbane Geraldo, an old-style band leader whose main connection with modern jazz was to sign up its young bloods for the Queen Mary's Orchestra.

Above: Baritone saxophonist supreme Gerry Mulligan was born in the New York on 6th April 1927, and worked with Gene Krupa and Claude Thornhill before leaving Thornhill to join up with Miles Davis for the sessions which led to 'The Birth Of The Cool'. In the next 40 years he had bands of his own in various formats, ranging from four to over twelve pieces.

music first hand (the latter point also applied to the traditionalists, but, of course, they had a host of records to study). To overcome these obstacles, some of the British musicians played in the bands carried by the trans-Atlantic liner, Queen Mary. These musicians went under the name of 'Geraldo's Navy' as the booking agent for the line was bandleader Geraldo. The Queen Mary was in dock in New York for perhaps 36 hours, during which time the sailor-musicians haunted 52nd Street, to see their heroes in the flesh.

Above: Victor Feldman, the Boy Wonder of page 99, now grown into a full-sized drummer, pianist and vibraharpist. Having worked with Ted Heath and Ronnie Scott in the 1940s, Feldman crossed the Atlantic to sign on with Woody Herman in 1955, later working as a session man on the West Coast.

Above: Dizzy Gillespie, seen here surrounded by excited British jazz fans and musicians (including Ronnie Scott, whose head is second to the right from Gillespie's), on a visit to Paris. Gillespie was a generous teacher, and, in contrast to many other jazzmen, who were intensely protective about their ideas and their technique being copied, he enjoyed passing on his knowledge to future generations in the greater interest of good music. He was also a great traveller, and made many 'official' tours on behalf of the United States Government – the first jazz musician to be nominated as a cultural representative.

As drummer Tony Crombie put it, 'It was a visual as well as an aural lesson in the new techniques'. As in the American scene, the British bop musicians permeated the dance bands and whether they liked the new sounds or not (mostly they didn't), the old guard bandleaders had to put up with it, if only because they had to consider a growing public for bebop. One of the old guard, Bert Ambrose (who had been leading a conventional dance band since the early 1920s), strongly objected to the use of the top cymbal, acidly enquiring 'Why the sound of frying?'

To play as they wished, a handful – not more than a dozen or so – of the young tyros met at a dingy rehearsal basement called Mac's Rehearsal Rooms, in Great Windmill Street, near Piccadilly in London. The participants included saxophonists Ronnie Scott, Johnny Dankworth, and Johnny Rogers; trumpeter Hank Shaw; pianists Bernie Fenton and Tommy Pollard; drummers Tony Crombie and Laurie Morgan; and bassists Lennie Bush and Joe Muddel. They called their venture the Club Eleven – ten musicians and a manager, Harry Morris. At first a private exercise, as at Minton's, it quickly aroused public curiosity, and British bebop was born. An independent label, Esquire, managed by drummer/collector Carlo Krahmer, was the first to record the rudimentary attempts by British musicians to master this new idiom from the United States.

Left: A cartoon advertisement for the Club 11 at 41 Great Windmill Street. Less a location, more a group of young jazz bloods who wanted to play bebop, the Club was, in fact, Mac's Rehearsal Room, an established practice hall. The founding musicians were Joe Muddel, Tony Crombie, Laurie Morgan, Johnny Dankworth, Hank Shaw, Tommy Pollard, Bernie Fenton, Ronnie Scott, Lennie Bush, and Johnny Rogers: the eleventh member was manager Harry Morris.

Below: A session at 41 Great Windmill Street. Ronnie Scott, tenor saxophone; Johnny Dankworth, alto saxophone; Tommy Pollard, piano; Lennie Bush, bass; Tony Crombie, drums.

The role of women in jazz has been primarily vocal, very often fronting the big bands, or working in smaller groups or as soloists accompanied by some of the finest musicians. The classic example is Bessie Smith, whose accompanists included Louis Armstrong.

The most famous of the singers other than Smith are Billie Holiday, Ella Fitzgerald, Sarah Vaughan, Dina Washington, and Carmen McRae.

Women have been prevented from excelling on many other jazz instruments because of the physical restrictions that seem to apply, particularly to their performance on the saxophone range and the trumpet. Of the piano, there have been some outstanding exponents, including Mary Lou Williams, Una Mae Carlisle, Marion McPartland, Shirley Scott, Lil Armstrong, Nellie Lutcher, and Rose Murphy; the last four were also excellent vocalists.

Right: Ella Fitzgerald was born in Virginia on 25th April 1918. Like Sarah Vaughan, her career was launched when she won an amateur singing contest at the Apollo Theatre, in Harlem. After being taken up by Tiny Bradshaw she joined Chick Webb, with whom she had her first million seller 'A-Tisket, A-Tasket', in 1938. She led the band when Webb died in the following year, after which she decided on a solo career. Her main employer was Norman Granz, who starred her in promotions all over the world, with material, ranging from jazz , through contemporary compositions, to the great works of Cole Porter and Jerome Kern.

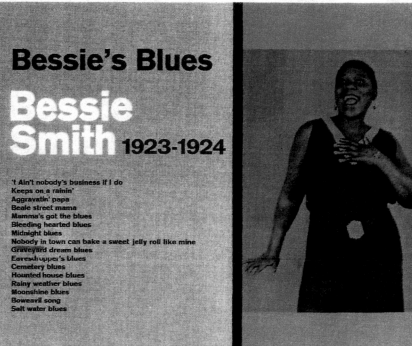

Classic Jazz masters

PHILIPS

Bessie's Blues

Bessie Smith 1923-1924

't Ain't nobody's business if I do
Keeps on a rainin'
Aggravatin' papa
Beale street mama
Mamma's got the blues
Bleeding hearted blues
Midnight blues
Nobody in town can bake a sweet jelly roll like mine
Graveyard dream blues
Eavesdropper's blues
Cemetery blues
Haunted house blues
Rainy weather blues
Moonshine blues
Boweavil song
Salt water blues

PHILIPS

Above left: Gertrude Pridgett – otherwise 'Ma' Rainey – was probably the first vocalist to transform the old blues style into a modern jazz idiom. She taught Bessie Smith.

Left: Bertha 'Chippie' Hill began her career with 'Ma' Rainey before going solo.

Above: Perhaps the greatest of them all, Bessie Smith was born in Tennessee on 15th April 1895. As 'Ma' Rainey was 'Mother' of the blues, Smith was its 'Empress'. She exceeded her tutor both in fame and fortune – becoming, in her prime, the highest paid black performer in the world.

Top left: Sarah Vaughan's career included work with some of the finest contemporary bands, including those of Billy Eckstine and Earl Hines.

Top right: Considered by many to fall into the category of blues rather than jazz, Billie Holiday's haunting voice defies such stereotyping and her inclusion in the jazz pantheon is more than justified by the number of fine jazz musicians who worked with her – including Benny Goodman, Roy Eldridge, Don Redman, and Benny Carter.

Left: Dinah Washington starred with Lionel Hampton; although she crossed over to mainstream music, she never neglected her jazz roots.

Above: Britain's finest, Cleo Laine.

A Rich Tapestry

During the 1950s and 1960s, bebop – gradually to be dignified by the term 'modern jazz' – established itself as a box office attraction, and its more talented and innovative exponents played clubs and concerts throughout the world, mostly in the West, but also in Asia and Australasia. They were also constantly in the recording studios. They had formally entered the jazz pantheon and were discussed by their followers with the same reverential tones as the traditionalists talked of King Oliver, Louis Armstrong, 'Jelly Roll' Morton, Sidney Bechet and Bix Beiderbecke.

Some of the recordings sold in their thousands. 'Take Five' by Dave Brubeck's Quartet, made in 1961, and 'Desifinado' by Stan Getz, with guitarist Charlie Byrd, made in 1962, each sold well in excess of one million copies. The advent of the long-playing record in the early 1950s enabled the musicians to stretch themselves more than they could within the limitations of the old 78rpm shellac with its duration of only three minutes or so (while, for the traditionalists, the LP made it possible for many old favourites, and many previously unissued 'takes', to appear in album compilations).

The new jazz was to have its boundaries extended by outstanding soloists like tenor saxophonists Sonny Rollins, John Coltrane and Wayne Shorter, and by the groups led by the bassist and composer Charles Mingus. Alto saxophonists Ornette Coleman and Eric Dolphy, and tenor saxophonist Albert Ayler, pushed the frontiers even further with a style that was described as 'free-form', which was a defiance of all the known conventions and which cast aside formal harmonies, predetermined chord sequences, key signatures and tonality. It was a sort of musical anarchy,

Above left: More than any other saxophonist, John Coltrane, assumed Parker's mantle of wayward greatness.

Below left: Brubeck's 'Take Five' sold over one million copies, became a standard in music of all types, and did much to establish the credibility of modern jazz.

Above: Theodore 'Sonny' Rollins was born in New York on 7th September 1929, and before he was 21 he had already played with future greats such as Ark Blakey, Miles Davis and Thelonious Monk. An innovative technician, he has rarely compromised to suit popular tastes.

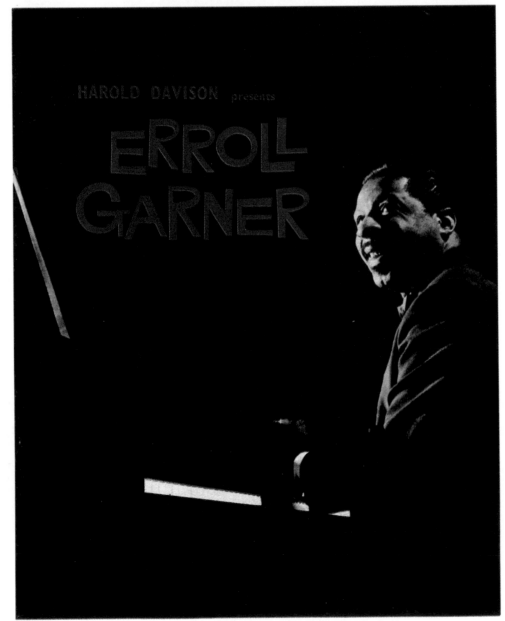

though it filled the minds and the pens of the critics more than it did the seats in clubs and concert halls.

The big white bands of Woody Herman and Stan Kenton and the black bands of Count Basie and Duke Ellington, virtually the only survivors of the big bands of the early 1950s, still flourished, although Basie had to temporarily abandon the big unit to form a sextet and even Ellington didn't always find the going easy. The cost of paying so many star musicians and their attendants' touring expenses became prohibitive and, in the Duke's case, he had to subsidize his orchestra with the enormous income he received from the royalties on the hundreds of tunes he had written.

Other big bands to join the circuit were those of Buddy Rich and the Thad Jones-Mel Lewis Orchestra. Rich, like Herman in his later days, used mainly young players straight from music schools, and did not carry the quota of outstanding soloists that characterized the big bands of the previous years. Ellington and Basie, however, managed to continue to employ improvizers of the highest quality.

Besides the club, theatre and concert hall circuit of the United States, the ever-increasing interest in jazz internationally gave bands and soloists employment in all parts of the world, most notably in Britain, Continental Europe and Japan. The great performers all toured: Duke Ellington, Count Basie, Woody Herman, Stan Kenton, Buddy Rich, each with a large orchestra. The enormous expense involved was justified by the receipts from countries that had been starved of jazz.

Above left: Bernard 'Buddy' Rich was born in New York on 30th September 1917. He was a prodigy, thrust into the limelight by his parents at eighteen months: by the age of eleven he had his own band. His jazz pedigree includes time with some of the finest white big bands of the day – Harry James', Artie Shaw's and Tommy Dorsey's – before he signed up with the outfit which ideally suited his extrovert showman talents – Jazz at the Philharmonic. Although he later had smaller groups of his own, he often returned to the big band formula.

Left: The much-loved Erroll Garner, a keyboard man with a style all of his own, advertized in this programme as the world's greatest jazz pianist.

Right: Norman Granz presents Gillespie.

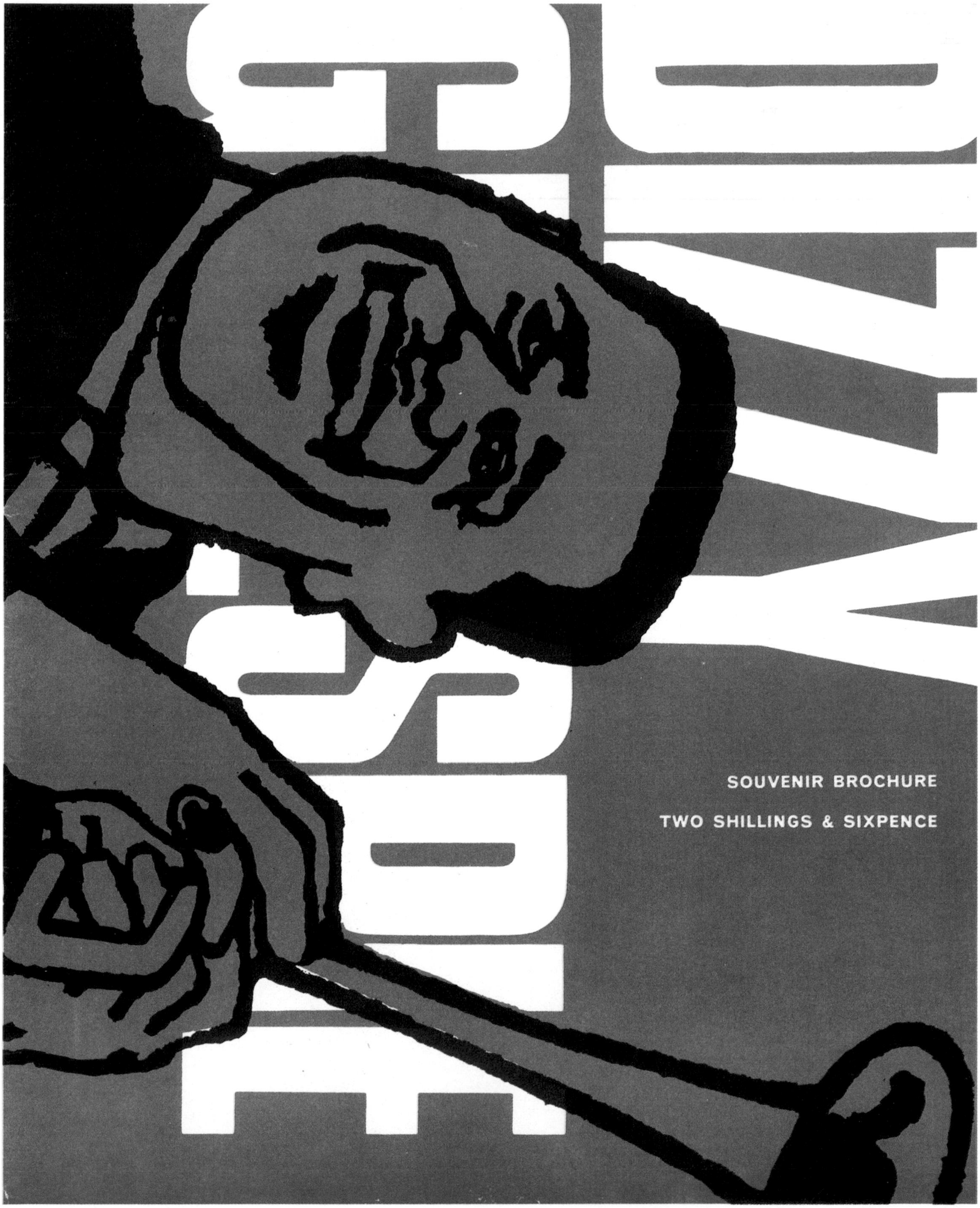
DIZZY
GILLESPIE
SOUVENIR BROCHURE
TWO SHILLINGS & SIXPENCE

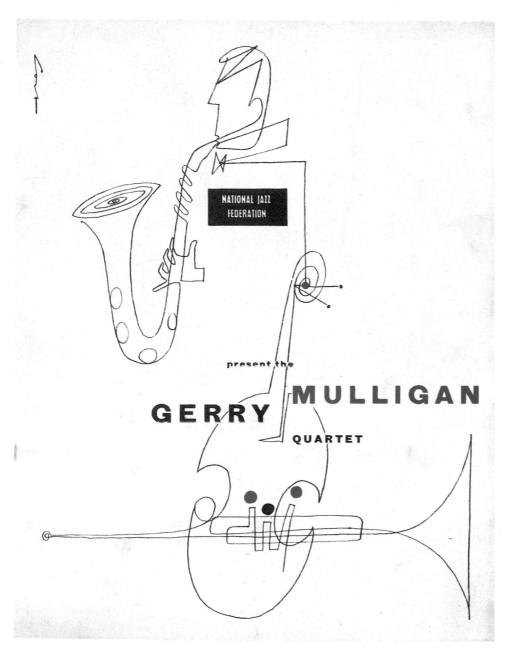

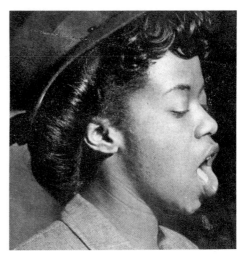

Above: The 'Divine' Sarah Vaughan, who was touring extensively in the 1950s.

Far left: A concert programme for an appearance by the Modern Jazz Quartet, on tour in Britain in 1957. In his programme notes, Raymond Horricks claims: 'Under the direction of John Lewis, The Modern Jazz Quartet has gained recognition as the most musically cohesive small group to appear in jazz since the 1948/9 Miles Davis band. It has proved to be an answer (and to my mind a more complete one than the Gerry Mulligan Quartet) to the doldrums of the late 1940s, when the unison ensemble small group dominated modern jazz.' The line-up for the tour was John Lewis, piano; Milt Jackson, vibes; Percy Heath, bass; and Connie Kay, drums.

Smaller units also toured, including the Modern Jazz Quartet, Jazz at the Philharmonic, and the various bands led by Stan Getz, Gerry Mulligan, and Dizzy Gillespie. In addition individual artistes such as the vocalists Sarah Vaughan, Ella Fitzgerald, Carmen McRae, Billie Holiday and Jimmy Rushing, travelled extensively. The recordings of all these musicians sold in their thousands globally.

On the traditional side, veteran performers continued to hold a place on the international stage. The George Lewis band, for example, toured Europe and Japan, while many soloists of the old school such as Wild Bill Davison toured singly, relying on the provision of capable, and sometimes even inspired, support from local bands that, within a few short years, had absorbed the idiom.

While no other European country had quite as many similarly-styled traditional bands, there was immense activity on the Continent, particularly exemplified by the bands of clarinettists Claude Luter and André Rewellioty, soprano saxophonist Pierre Braslavsky, and pianist Claude Bolling in France (all of these playing and recording with Sidney Bechet), the Swing College Band led by multi-instrumentalist Peter Schilperoot in Holland (who also recorded with Bechet, and with violinist Joe Venuti, pianist Teddy Wilson, ex-Bob Crosby trumpeter Billy Butterfield, and singer Jimmy Witherspoon from the United States), trumpeter Papa Bue's Viking Jazz Band from Denmark, the Cave Stompers from Sweden, and the Big Chief Jazz Band from Norway.

Australia produced Graeme Bell's Australian Jazz Band, Frank Coughlan's Dixielanders, Keith Hounslow's Jazz Hounds, Frank Johnson's Fabulous Dixielanders, the Port Jackson Jazz Band, the Southern Jazz Group, and the Yarra City Stompers. Graeme Bell's Band recorded with Ellington trumpeter Rex Stewart and Condon trumpeter Max Kaminsky and was the first Australian band to tour internationally, making their first trip in 1947 on a very low budget. In 1948 they brought to the London jazz scene a breezy non-conformist attitude that did much to transform the atmosphere of jazz clubs: before their arrival it had been the practice to sit and listen and nod heads to jazz, but 'The Bells' urged people to dance, and the resulting number of cash customers not necessarily interested in jazz was to have a profound and

Above: Trumpeter/vocalist/guitarist Ken Colyer was born in Norfolk, England, on 18th April 1928. He steeped himself in the genuine music of New Orleans from an early age, and later, when a seaman, jumped ship in America to visit the shrine in person. There he worked with George Lewis until he was deported. Returning to Britain he founded a traditionalist ensemble, with which he continued to tour for over 30 years. Though ranking equal in status with Barber, Bilk and Ball among British traditionalists, he stood to one side of the 'Trad' boom.

Left: Clarinettist Bernard 'Acker' Bilk was born in Somerset on 28th January 1929, and he worked with Ken Colyer's band early in his career. He founded his own group in the late 1950s, and his early recording successes did much to bring 'Trad' to a wider audience: this was to start a boom that made Bilk and fellow 'Three B' bandleaders Chris Barber and Kenny Ball household names around the world.

Left: Trumpeter/vocalist/bandleader Kenny Ball profitted from the surge in interest in 'Trad' music with popular hits such as 'March Of The Siamese Children', 'So Do I', and 'Midnight in Moscow', while simultaneously preserving his band's credibility amongst the jazz fraternity by maintaining one of the highest standards of excellence of any British Dixieland ensemble of the period. Ball supported Armstrong on his visit to London in 1968, and although his mainstream popularity waned slightly after the 'Trad' boom subsided, he continued to work in TV and variety – including Royal Command Performances – and remained a household name.

Right: Chris Barber's successes during 'Trad's' heyday in the early 1960s included 'Petite Fleur', 'Whistling Rufus', 'Hushabye', and 'Bobby Shafto', and it was Barber who launched Lonnie Donegan on his solo career when 'Rock Island Line', which was in fact recorded for a Barber album, became a smash hit. Like Ball and Bilk, Barber, although content to benefit from the excesses of 'Trad' popularity, was in fact a fine and serious musician; he took 'Trad's' passing in his stride and reverted to one of his first loves, the blues, with a mixed repertoire jazz and blues band which led him into another 30 years of successful recording and performing.

beneficial effect on the economics of jazz promotion.

In the late 1950s and early 1960s there erupted a purely British phenomenon, 'Trad'. It was a commercialization of traditionalism, with an emphasis on the vaudeville elements: hand-clapping to a rigid beat, throaty vocals *à la* Louis Armstrong, and eccentric dress. The latter was a highly successful ploy in the case of Acker Bilk and his Paramount Jazz Band, who attired themselves in an Edwardian costume of narrow-bottomed trousers, pin-striped waistcoats, string ties and curly-brimmed bowler hats. Others aped the gimmick.

The commercial success of Trad was due, in no small way, to the Hit Parade successes of Chris Barber with 'Petit Fleur' (1959), Acker Bilk with 'Stranger on the Shore' (1961), and Kenny Ball with 'Midnight in Moscow' (1961). In this extraordinary bonanza, (a most unexpected throw-back to the pioneering endeavours of George Webb's Dixielanders), the Crane River Jazz Band and Humphrey Lyttelton's first band were among some forty fully professional bands on the road playing Trad, with some many hundreds more joining in the merry-go-round in a semi-professional capacity.

The basement at 100 Oxford Street, which had first become a jazz club in 1941 with the Feldman Swing Club sessions on Sunday nights, turned into the London Jazz Club in 1949 when the Wilcox brothers took it over. It later became the Humphrey Lyttelton Club, open seven nights a week, from 1952 to 1959. Finally it became the 100 Club and has been

operating under this title ever since.

Eventually the advent of 'Merseybeat', led by the Beatles from Liverpool, and the rise to fame of the Rolling Stones from Richmond, Surrey, established a train of events that led to the collapse of Trad in the 1960s, although some of the bands survived, notably the Three Bs (Ball, Barber and Bilk); Alex Welsh (until his death in June 1982); the intransigent traditionalist trumpeter Ken Colyer (who died in 1989); and Humphrey Lyttelton (though with a substantial change in style and policy to that with which he started in 1948). The death of Trad was the end of another epoch in jazz history.

In Britain and on the Continent, as in America, bebop, which had begun as a private, almost clandestine, exercise, became 'commercial' and by the early 1950s

there were several 'modern' bands on the road, including those of accordionist Tito Burns, alto saxophonist Johnny Dankworth, tenor saxophonist Ronnie Scott, pianist Ralph Sharon, drummer Tony Crombie, tenor saxophonist Don Rendell, tenor saxophonist Tubby Hayes, and Ted Heath's Big Band featuring the young bebop bloods in carefully measured allocations of solos.

Many notable musicians from the Continent, in particular Scandinavia, played in the modern style: alto saxophonist Arne Domnerus from Sweden, trumpeter Rob Pronk, singer Rita Reys and pianist/singer Pia Beck from Holland, tenor saxophonist Bobby Jaspar and harmonica player Toots Thielemans from Belgium, and trumpeter Rolf Ericson from Denmark. Bebop, like traditional jazz and swing music, had become an international language.

In 1959 Ronnie Scott opened his own club at 39 Gerrard Street, a somewhat rundown thoroughfare near Leicester Square in what is now London's Chinatown. With only limited facilities (they had no liquor licence), and featuring only British jazzmen, the venture was financially disastrous. It was only by booking American soloists (backed by increasingly adept British players), commencing in 1961 with the tenor saxophonist Zoot Sims, that the club became commercially successful. However much non-American

Above left: Tenor saxophonist Edward 'Tubby' Hayes was born in London on 30th January 1935, and made his early living as a musician with the big bands of Ambrose and Jack Parnell. He founded an octet in 1955, moving up, by way of his joint leadership of the Jazz Couriers with Ronnie Scott in the late 1950s, to a big band in the 1960s. He caught the imagination of a wider public, and made many TV programmes and films which did not necessarily place a heavy accent on jazz music. He was, however, justifiably taken seriously by American contemporaries, guested with Ellington, and led several units featuring American musicians who were sympathetic to the progressive style he wished to play. Hayes died in 1973 at a tragically early age.

Left: George Melly in fine form.

Right: Ted Heath with his band. It was a fine breeding ground for the young bebop bloods of the day.

Right: Trombonist/bandleader Ted Heath had a distinguished jazz history, and was in fact a featured soloist on the first-ever recording reviewed by Edgar Jackson in the *Melody Maker* in 1926 – 'Riverboat Shuffle' by Jack Hylton's Kit Kat band. Although advertized as a 'hot' band in the 1950s, and regarded as such by its many non-jazz fans, it was really a heavily arranged 'swing' orchestra. While Heath employed many young musicians with progressive yearnings, it was because they were the most talented, not because of the style they espoused, and their ideas were as much frustrated as they were nurtured by Heath's format.

jazzmen had developed their skills, the superiority of the Americans, and their consequent drawing power, remained.

By the mid-1950s a further new 'movement' had emerged to give jazz yet another category of style. Called 'mainstream', as it pursued a middle road, it was neither traditionalism nor modernism. Its leading figure in Britain was trumpeter Humphrey Lyttelton who jettisoned his highly successful and traditional format in favour of

B E N W E B S T E R

PLAYS BALLADS

STORYVILLE
SLP-4118

The high and mighty Hawk

Coleman Hawkins

Above and left: Ben Webster and Coleman Hawkins were regular travellers to Europe. Webster played with an enormous range of bands, including, principally, Duke Ellington's. As a touring soloist, his music was revered around the world.

In the early years of jazz, Hawkins, rivalled only by Lester Young, was the master of the saxophone, and an influence on all his contemporaries. Although challenged later by Parker in terms of overall saxophone virtuosity, he lays claim to being the greatest of the tenors.

Above: Canadian pianist Oscar Peterson was influenced early in his career by Nat 'King' Cole, and later by Art Tatum. Born in 1925, he spent his formative years leading trios. In later days he toured as a soloist with pick-up support, although he has often worked with Martin Drew and Niels-Henning Orsted Pedersen. Admired for his free-wheeling style and the sheer number of notes he squeezes in, he has managed to build a popular mainstream career covering classic melodies, while never neglecting his jazz heritage.

bands that included the saxophone and that made use of harmonized arrangements rather than employing collective improvization.

The English critic Stanley Dance, resident in America, organized a series of sessions that bore the 'mainstream' tag and featured, among others, the ex-Count Basie trumpeter Buck Clayton, who toured Britain several times with the Humphrey Lyttelton Band.

In December 1965 Ronnie Scott moved from the dingy basement of 39 Gerrard Street to more opulent premises in Frith Street, Soho, and with more space and better facilities was able to feature a stream of famous jazz names. These included saxophonists Roland Kirk, Johnny Griffin, Stan Getz, Yusef Lateef, Ben Webster,

Bud Freeman, Sonny Rollins, Dexter Gordon, George Coleman, Lee Konitz, and Warne Marsh; trumpeters Freddy Hubbard, Miles Davis, Dizzy Gillespie, and Charlie Shavers; pianists Earl Hines, Horace Silver, Bill Evans, Oscar Peterson, and Mary Lou Williams, as well as a host of other soloists; this was in addition to the bands of Count Basie, Woody Herman, Harry James, the Kenny Clarke-Francy Boland Band from France, and the Buddy Rich Orchestra. Such an influx, in London or any of the other capital cities of the world, would not have been envisaged ten years earlier. In October 1989 Scott, and his partner Pete King, celebrated thirty continuous years of running a jazz club, although not without a number of crises that brought them near to closure.

JAZZ IN PRINT

As in America, enthusiasts produced magazines in their homes, although the British 'publishers' had enormous problems with the authorities who rationed paper during and after the war. Their enthusiasm overcame the shortages and many crusading broadsheets appeared, the pride of place belonging to *Jazz Music*, edited and published by Max Jones and Albert McCarthy of the Jazz Sociological Society, working from Jones' home in Primrose Hill, North London.

In the early 1980s, after gradually running down its jazz coverage for several years, the *Melody Maker*, which had been the first magazine in the world to champion jazz, abandoned itself entirely to rock'n'roll in its various manifestations. Until this departure in policy it had the longest standing record of support for the music. 'The cause' no longer has a weekly paper as it once did in the shape of both the *Melody Maker* and the *Musical Express* (which abandoned its jazz coverage in the mid-1970s), but a significant number of monthly magazines still provide the buff with a ceaseless flow of news, features, discographies and biographies. These include *Jazz Journal*, founded in 1950 by Sinclair Traill (who died in 1983) and now owned and edited by Eddie Cook; *Jazz Express*, owned by hotelier Peter Boizot; *Wire*, owned by publisher Naim Atallah; *Jazz Rag*, published in Birmingham; and *Jazz At Ronnie Scott's*, primarily a house magazine, but encompassing coverage of events and features unconnected with the club. The Mouldy Fygge is catered for by *Storyville* magazine, edited by Laurie Wright, and *New Orleans*, edited by Mike Hazeldine. The last two are redolent of the crop of revivalist magazines published in the 1940s and are labours of love. They examine in depth the most obscure (and often musically worthless) musicians, and their writers resolutely ignore modern trends.

From the mid-1970s or thereabouts there has been greater media acceptance of jazz, and even in the quality daily and Sunday papers, record reviews, news items and obituaries are common, in marked contrast to the past era when any mention of a jazzman was an event and usually highly inaccurate. In association with JAZZ FM (see below), *The Observer* has produced a glossy quarterly, edited by Tony Russell.

Above and right: Jazz has always inspired a committed, perhaps even fanatical, following of enthusiasts who like nothing better than to chart and discuss the minutiae of their beloved idiom. For this reason many of the magazines and journals published are little more than newsheets or circulars, passed out among discrete groups involved in particular specialities. On another level there are professionally produced magazines which favour one type of music over another – examples of these are the separate groups of publications that sprouted during the traditional versus modernist debate, backing one side or the other. There are also variations in style and approach, from the text-heavy, small print journals, swathed in footnotes and discographical material, which are academic in approach, to the glossy, glamorous, lavish productions, in which the pictures are given much more emphasis than the words. Finally, there are mainstream magazines which are not specifically jazz-oriented, but which cover it sporadically as a lifestyle subject when fashion, and the mood, dictates. The one thing that all categories have in common is that they provide rich pickings for the collector of ephemera – whether the casual snapper-up of unconsidered trifles, or the true jazz archivist. Much of the material in this book comes from such sources, proving what a valuable database they can provide.

NEW STATESMAN
SOCIETY

The new jazz age

André Gorz: An essay on Thatcher's dependency economy

The Baltic uprisings: John Lloyd reports

Christmas Books: Sheila Rowbotham, George Melly, Jenny Diski, Hanif Kureishi

Young black musicians in Britain are reclaiming jazz for their generation. They play jazz that's savvy, sharp and serious, with roots in hard bop and hip hop, rap and reggae. Don't invoke the y-word. This music is strictly for the kids

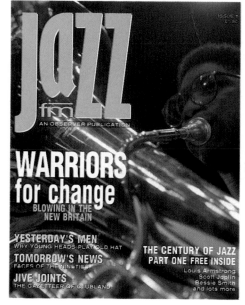

ISSUE 1

JAZZ
fm
AN OBSERVER PUBLICATION

WARRIORS
for change
BLOWING IN THE NEW BRITAIN

YESTERDAY'S MEN
WHY YOUNG HEADS PLAY OLD HAT

TOMORROW'S NEWS
FACES OF THE NINETIES

JIVE JOINTS
THE GAZETTEER OF CLUBLAND

THE CENTURY OF JAZZ PART ONE FREE INSIDE
Louis Armstrong
Scott Joplin
Bessie Smith
and lots more

JAZZ ON THE AIR

In March 1990, a British pianist, David Lee, and a wealthy consortium gained a franchise from the Independent Broadcasting Authority to broadcast jazz 24 hours a day, seven days a week on a British radio station which they called JAZZ FM. As was expected, a commercial station, depending upon advertizing for its revenue, could not ignore middle-of-the-road material, a policy that enraged the traditionalists.

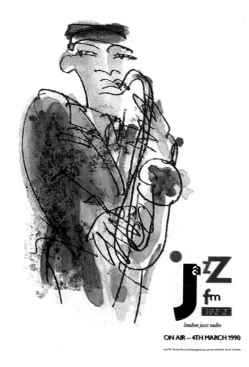

JAZZ
fm
102·2
tuneless jazz radio

ON AIR – 4TH MARCH 1990

Storyville 31

October – November 1970   3s.

Adelaide Hall – the Singing Blackbird

Territory Bands in Britain and the U.S.A.

THIS ISSUE INCREASED TO 32 PAGES – THE PRINT RUN INCREASED TO 16,000
THIS MAGAZINE IS FREE! PLEASE TAKE ONE ... and some for your friends if you wish   No. 59

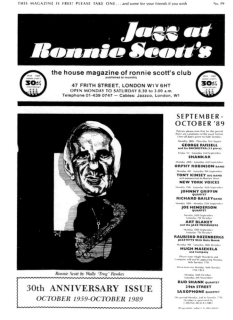

Jazz at Ronnie Scott's

the house magazine of ronnie scott's club
published bi-monthly

47 FRITH STREET, LONDON W1V 6HT
OPEN MONDAY TO SATURDAY 8.30 to 3.00 a.m.
Telephone 01-439 0747 — Cables: Jazzco, London, W1

SEPTEMBER-
OCTOBER '89

Ronnie Scott by Wally 'Trog' Fawkes

30th ANNIVERSARY ISSUE
OCTOBER 1959-OCTOBER 1989

THE
BIG BAND YEARS

BRUCE CROWTHER
MIKE PINFOLD
Picture Editor
FRANKLIN S. DRIGGS

THE **GUINNESS**
JAZZ A-Z

JAZZ TERMS JAZZ PEOPLE JAZZ EVENTS
JAZZ PLACES JAZZ NICKNAMES

EXPLAINED BY PETER CLAYTON
AND PETER GAMMOND

GUINNESS BOOKS

MINGUS
A CRITICAL BIOGRAPHY
BRIAN PRIESTLEY

DISCOGRAPHY

For a music that, despite its media appeal has remained a minority interest, there is a quite astonishing number of recordings, on 78s, albums, and now CDs. These run into hundreds of thousands and most are documented in meticulous detail in a selection of discographies, commencing with *Hot Discography* by Charles Delaunay in 1936. These were followed by *Index to Jazz* by Orin Blackstone (1944); *Jazz Directory* by Dave Carey, Albert McCarthy and Ralph Venables (1950); *Jazz Records 1897–1942* by Brian Rust; *Jazz Records 1942–65* by Jorgen Jepsen; and latterly, *Jazz Records 1965 to 1980* by Eric Raben. The nature of this beast is that as discographers toil, daily their work becomes out of date.

LITERATURE

The amount of literature devoted to jazz has been enormous. It has been estimated that there are well over a thousand volumes on the subject, with no sign of the output abating. Among the more notable contributions are *Jazz Hot* by Hughes Pannassiè; *Jazzmen* by Frederic Ramsey and Charles Edward Smith; *American Jazz Music* by Wilder Hobson; *Really the Blues* by Mezz Mezzrow (with Bernard Wolfe); *Shining Trumpets* by Rudi Blesh; *Bird Lives* by Ross Russell; *The Encyclopedia of Jazz* by Leonard Fuller, and *Dinosaurs in the Morning* by Whitney Balliat.

Europe's contribution to the literature has been exceptional: foremost among many fine books are *The Best of Jazz: Basin Street to Harlem* (part 1), and *The Best of Jazz : Enter The Giants* (part 2), by Humphrey Lyttelton; *Miles Davis*, by Ian Carr; *Mingus*, by Brian Priestley; *Bechet: The Wizard of Jazz; Song Of The Hawk;* (a biography of Coleman Hawkins), and the *Who's Who Of Jazz* (an encyclopedia of over 1,000 musicians), all by the trumpeter John Chilton; *Jazz: The Essential Companion*, by Ian Carr, Digby Fairweather, and Brian Priestley; and, from Germany, *Jazz: A Photo History*, by Joachim-Ernst Berendt.

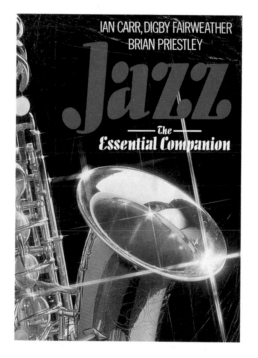

Left and above: Hundreds of books are published about jazz every year around the world: their range reflects the breadth of publishing in general. There are 'lifestyle' books, which are little more than coffee-table items, in which the beautiful pictures are designed to disguise the paucity of information they contain. Then there are academic treatises — packed full of tiny specific facts which have hardly any relevance to jazz as it is played and enjoyed, and even less with the broader world which exists outside the idiom. There are biographies, dictionaries, encyclopedias, discographies, sociological examinations, and even practical books on how to do it! Again, the unifying theme is that they are all about jazz, and although they may range from the hideously esoteric to the hopelessly general, they are a treasure house for the dedicated collector and gatherer of ephemera, to whom no book on the subject should prove uninteresting.

JAZZ ON THE SCREEN

A development of the 1980s is the jazz video, many of the compilations including vintage footage as well as contemporary film. A major corporation, Warner Bros, produced two significant films based on the lives of jazzmen – 'Round Midnight', based on the life of, and starring, tenor saxophonist Dexter Gordon, and 'Bird', produced and directed by Clint Eastwood. Other landmark productions are 'Thelonious', a documentary based on the life of pianist Thelonious Monk and 'Let's Get Lost', a filmic collage of Chet Baker's life.

Historically jazz has not been well-served by the film world. Until recently it was largely ignored as a subject, but when it was dealt with, the treatment has generally been so crass as to be laughable. An example from this book illustrates the patronizing, condescending, and downright misleading attitude that has normally been adopted: 'New Orleans Story', a real opportunity to allow legendary performers such as Bigard and Armstrong to assist in the documentation of their tradition, was instead turned into a light-hearted musical which said nothing about the roots of jazz.

Fortunately the trend is one of improvement, and several films in the past few years have covered jazz in a realistic, unglamorized way which has contributed mightily to the greater understanding of the music and the people who make it.

In particular, *Round Midnight*, an exceptional film work from French Director Bertrand Tavernier, tells the story, bleakly, but sympathetically, of an ageing, alcoholic American tenor saxophonist on a working visit to Paris. The storyline could be based on the life of any number of famous jazzmen: there are elements from the history of the man who actually starred in the film, Dexter Gordon, but it could equally well be describing the later years of Ben Webster or Coleman Hawkins. Above all, the style is realistic in the extreme, revealing the deprivations and loneliness of the musician's life, without attempting to emphasize or create a non-existent glamour.

In addition, *Bird*, Clint Eastwood's life of Charlie Parker, featuring a stunning central performance by Forest Whitaker, illustrated that here, at last, is a mainstream film director who is prepared to take the subject seriously.

EPHEMERA COLLECTIONS

An important and interesting development to arise from the New Orleans renaissance is the enormous amount of jazz ephemera now to be found in the Louisiana State Museum (71 Chartres Street, Amistad Research Centre, Tilton Hall, 6823 St Charles Avenue, New Orleans), and the Howard-Tilton Memorial Library (part of Tulane University, 7001 Freret Street, New Orleans). Between them, these institutions house tens of thousands of recordings, on 78s, EPs, LPs, reel-to-reel tapes, cylinders and piano rolls, together with a huge archive of sheet music, literature, playbills, programmes, paintings, photographs and other memorabilia. The principal collection in the Howard-Tilton Library is the William Ransom Hogan Jazz Archive, begun in 1957 by the historian Dr William Ransom Hogan with the help of a grant from the Ford Foundation.

Call it what you will, ephemera comes in a thousand different shapes and forms, many of which have been illustrated throughout this volume. Many types, including rare record sleeves, 78rpm records, posters, concert programmes, and even tickets and membership cards, can gain considerable extrinsic value outside of the importance they have to the collector.

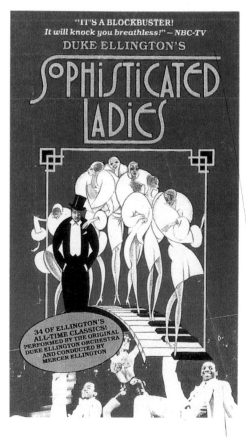

JAZZ LOSSES

Internationally, the jazz scene resembled an enormous tapestry: some of the threads thick and of brilliant colours, others pale and thin, some intertwining and some quite separate in the overall pattern. But as the colours and strands of the tapestry altered year by year, so many of those who fashioned it died. Regularly, the announcements of departures saddened the jazz fraternity.

Bix Beiderbecke died in 1931 and King Oliver in 1938, long before either was fully acknowledged, and from 1940 (when the music was beginning to be thoroughly documented) others were to pass on. Some, like Johnny Dodds (1940), and 'Jelly Roll' Morton (1941), would, had they survived, have assuredly seen a revival in their fortunes. Morton died in poverty and Dodds was running an apartment block in Chicago. Others who died were Bunny Berigan (1942), Jimmy Noone (1944), Bunk Johnson (1949), Fletcher Henderson (1952), Tommy Dorsey (1956), Jimmy Dorsey (1957), Sidney Bechet, Billie Holiday and Lester Young (1959), Jack Teagarden (1964), Muggsy Spanier, Red Allen and Ed Hall (1967), George Lewis (1968), Pee Wee Russell (1969), Johnny Hodges (1970), Louis Armstrong (1971), Kid Ory and Gene Krupa (1973), Duke Ellington (1974), Barney Bigard (1980), Harry James (1983), Count Basie (1984), Benny Goodman (1986), Woody Herman (1987), and Wild Bill Davison (1990) – the latter working almost up to his death at the age of 82.

Losses from the modernist side included Fats Navarro (1950), Charlie Parker (1955), Clifford Brown (1956), Bud Powell (1966), Charles Mingus and Stan Kenton (1979), Art Pepper (1982), Zoot Sims and Kenny Clark (1985), and Buddy Rich (1987, after battling against successive heart operations and returning to action in each case in an incredibly short space of time), Chet Baker and Gil Evans (1988), Mel Lewis (1989) and Sarah Vaughan and Dexter Gordon (1990).

In Britain, jazz's losses have included Phil Seaman (1972), Tubby Hayes (1973), Sandy Brown (1975), and Ken Colyer (1989). During his short life (he died aged 46), Sandy Brown, arguably the most brilliant clarinet player Britain has ever produced, calculated on a computer that the average life-span of a jazz musician is 43 years. When he arrived at this deduction at the age of 44, he joked, 'I'm living on borrowed time'.

This page (clockwise from top left): Bix Beiderbecke, great white trumpeter and jazz genius, who died, largely unacknowledged, in 1931; King Oliver, trumpeter, one of the central figures in the early New Orleans days, and a strong influence on Armstrong, died 1938; Barney Bigard, clarinettist, who lived long enough to experience renewed fame during the revival, died 1980; and 'Jelly Roll' Morton, pianist, who traced his musical origins back to the place where jazz was born in the backstreets and sporting houses of the Crescent City, died 1941.

Right hand page (clockwise from top right): Count Basie, pianist, who led bands for nearly fifty years, died 1984; Duke Ellington, pianist, and perhaps the greatest of all big band leaders, died 1974; Emil Lacoume, no great musician, but a man whose jazz roots were planted in the nineteenth century, and whose activites are recorded in the earliest annals of the idiom, died 1946; Nat 'King' Cole, pianist, 1965; 'Fats' Waller, pianist, one of the most colourful 'characters' that jazz has thrown up, died 1943; and, finally, the greatest of them all, Louis Armstrong, trumpeter, singer, bandleader, and, above all, entertainer, whose passing in 1971 ended an era.

A LOOK TO THE FUTURE

A century after its birth the essential pulse of jazz, in a variety of styles, is to be found in the playing of many highly talented young musicians, principally in the United States and Britain. Andy Sheppard (**below**), Courtney Pine (**right**) and Loose Tubes (**below right**) are already established stars of the new generation, and Christopher Hollyday, Rick Margitza, Greg Osby, Roy Hargrove, Marcus Roberts, Rene Rosness and Terri-Lyn Carrington are excellent prospects.

But the continuing death toll among those who shaped the idiom's history and gave it romance is an inescapable fact. All of the big band leaders and most of their sidemen have died, as have virtually all the pioneers of traditional jazz. The revivalists of the 1940s are now well into their 60s, and there are no young players following in their footsteps. Only a handful of survivors of the bebop era have continued playing into the 1990s – Dizzy Gillespie, Miles Davis, and Stan Getz among them – and, it has to be said, the up-and-coming young players sadly lack the panache and glamour – and the stamp of originality – that characterized their predecessors. Across the stylistic board there are no Louis Armstrongs, 'Jelly Roll' Mortons or Duke Ellingtons; no Bix Beiderbeckes or Benny Goodmans.

However, to counterbalance this somewhat gloomy view, the wealth of recorded music now being released is enormous, and future generations will have the benefit of a comprehensive and exhaustive documentation of a unique and vibrant idiom that has impinged on public consciousness to an extent that the doughty pioneers in New Orleans could not possibly have envisaged.

Bibliography

Allen, Walter: *Hendersonia* (New Jersey; Highland Park, 1973)

Allen, Walter, with Brian Rust, revised by Laurie Wright: *King Oliver* (London; Storyville Publications, 1974, 1987)

Armstrong, Louis: *Satchmo* (London; Jazz Book Club, 1957)

Asbury, Herbert: *The French Quarter* (New York, Pocket Books, 1936)

Balliett, Whitney: *Dinosaurs in the Morning* (London; Jazz Book Club, 1962)

Baron, Stanley: *Benny, King of Swing* (London; Thames and Hudson, 1979)

Berendt, Joachim-Ernst: *Jazz: A Photo-History* (London; Andre Deutsch, 1979)

Blesh, Rudi: *Shining Trumpets* (New York; Alfred Knopf, 1946)

Boulton, David: *Jazz in Britain* (London; W. H. Allen, 1958)

Brunn, H. O.: *The Story of the Original Dixieland Jazz Band* (London: Jazz Book Club/Sidgwick and Jackson, 1963)

Calloway, Cab: *Of Minnie the Moocher and Me* (New York; Thos. Crowell)

Carey, Dave, with Albert McCarthy and Ralph Venables: *Jazz Directory, Vols 1–6* (Hampshire; Delphic Press and London; Cassell, 1950–55)

Carr, Ian: *Miles Davis* (London; Paladin, 1984)

Carr, Ian, with Digby Fairweather and Brian Priestley: *Jazz: The Essential Companion* (London; Grafton Books, 1987)

Chilton, John: *Who's Who of Jazz* (London; Macmillan, 1985

Chilton, John, with Max Jones: *Louis* (London; Studio Vista, 1971); *Sidney Bechet, The Wizard of Jazz* (London; Macmillan, 1987); *The Song of the Hawk; the Life and Recordings of Coleman Hawkins* (London; Quartet, 1990); *McKinney's Cotton Pickers* (London; Bloomsbury, 1978)

Clayton, Peter, with Peter Gammond; *Guinness Jazz A-Z* (later retitled *Guinness Jazz Companion*) (London; Guinness Superlatives, 1989)

Collier, James Lincoln: *Duke Ellington* (London, Michael Joseph)

Crowther, Bruce, and Mike Pinfold: *The Big Band Years* (Newton Abbot; David and Charles, 1988)

Dance, Stanley: *World of Earl Hines* (New York; Charles Scribner's, 1977)

Delaunay, Charles: *Hot Discography* (Paris; 1936 + reprints)

Feather, Leonard: *The Encyclopedia of Jazz* (London; Arthur Barker, 1961 + reprints)

Fernett, Gene: *Swing Out* (Michigan; Pendell Co. 1967)

Fox, Ted: *Showtime at the Apollo* (London; Quartet Books, 1983)

Godbolt, Jim: *All This and 10%* (London; Robert Hale, 1974); updated to *All This and Many a Dog* (London; Quartet, 1986)

Godbolt, Jim: *A History of Jazz in Britain 1919–50* (London; Quartet Books, 1984)

Godbolt, Jim: *A History of Jazz in Britain, 1950–70* (London; Quartet Books, 1989)

Goddard, Chris: *Jazz Away From Home* (London; Paddington Press)

Gordon, Max: *Live at the Village Vanguard* (New York; Da Capo Press)

Gottleib, Bill: *Golden Age of Jazz* (London; Quartet Books, 1979)

Grime, Kitty: *Jazz at Ronnie Scott's* (London; Robert Hale, 1979)

Harris, Rex: *Jazz* (Harmondsworth; Pelican, 1952)

Haskins, Jim: *The Cotton Club* (London; Robson Books, 1977)

Hobson, Wilder: *American Jazz Music* (London; Dent, 1940)

Hughes, Spike: *Opening Bars* (London; Museum Press, 1946)

Jepson, Jorgan Grunnett: *Jazz Records 1942–65* (Denmark; Holte, 1960–65)

Jewell, Derek: *A Portrait of Duke Ellington* (London; Pavilion, 1986)

Jones, Max: *Talking Jazz* (London; Macmillan, 1987)

Keepnews, Orrin, and Bill Grauer: *Pictorial History of Jazz* (London: Spring Books, 1960)

Kernfeld, Barry (ed): *The New Grove Dictionary of Jazz, Vols 1–2* (London; Macmillan, 1988)

Lyttelton, Humphrey: *The Best of Jazz – Basin Street to Harlem* (London; Robson Books, 1981)

Lyttelton, Humphrey: *The Best of Jazz – Enter the Giants* (London; Robson Books, 1981)

Meeker, Davis: *Jazz in the Movies* (London; Talisman Books, 1981)

Mezzrow, Mezz, with Bernard Wolfe: *Really the Blues* (New York; Random House, 1945)

Panassiè, Hughes: *Le Jazz Hot* (Paris; 1935 + reprints)

Priestley, Brian: *Mingus; A Critical Biography* (London; Quartet Books, 1984)

Ramsey, Frederic Jr, and Charles Edward Smith: *Jazzmen* (New York; Harcourt Brace Jovanovich, 1939)

Reisner, Robert: *Bird: The Legend of Charlie Parker* (London; Quartet Books, 1962)

Rose, Al, and Edmond Souchon: *New Orleans Jazz – Family Album* (New Orleans; Louisiana State University Press, 1967)

Rosenthal, G, and F. Zachery: *Jazzways* (1946)

Rust, Brian: *Jazz Records 1897–1942, Vols 1–2* (Essex; Storyville Publications)

Stuart, Jay Allison: *Call Him George* (London; Jazz Book Club, 1961)

Index

Acker Bilk and his Paramount Jazz Band, *142*, 143
Allen, Red, 46, 104, 154
Ambrose, Bert, 95, 132
Anderson, Tom, 13
    establishments of, *13, 16*
Ansermet, Ernest, 60
Armstrong, Lil, 134
Armstrong, Louis, 12, *15, 28, 29, 33*, 82, 96, 104, *110*, 154
    bands, 46, *48*
    biography, *117*
    birthplace of, *12*
    Britain, in, 71, 89, 91, *119*
    Fletcher Henderson's Orchestra, in, 42
    Hot Five, *35*, 41, 68
    Hot Seven, 41, 68
    King Oliver's Creole Jazz Band, with, 36
    Scandinavia, in, 75
Asmussen, Svend, 75
Asbury, Herbert, 11
Austin High School Gang, The, *39*
Ayler, Albert, 137

Bailey, Buster, 42
Bailey's Lucky Seven, *24*
Baker, Chet, 123, 154
Ball, Kenny, *101, 143*, 143
Barber, Chris, *101, 143*, *143*
Barnet, Charlie, 76, 77, 84
Basie, Count, 84, 86, *87*, 138, 154
Bebop, 119–133, 137, 144
Bechet, Sydney, *33*, 58, *59*, 60, *74*, 75, 104, 107, *114*, 115, 116, 141, 154
Beck, Pia, 144
Beiderbecke, Bix, 38, *47*, 51, 66, 68, 154
Bell, Graeme, *117*
Bennie Moten and his Orchestra, *49*
Bennie Peyton's Jazz Kings, *59*
Benny Pollack's Orchestra, *46*
Berigan, Bunny, 80, 154
Bert Firman's Rhythmic Eight, *66*, 68, *70*
Best of Jazz, The, 23
Bexleyheath and District Rhythm Club, 112
Big Chief Jazz Band, 141
Bigard, Barney, 42, 45, *110*, 154
Bilk, Acker, *101, 142*, 143
Bix and his Rhythm Jugglers, 38, *39*
Bix Beiderbecke and his Gang, 68
Black Swan Records, 41
Blake, Cyril, 98
Blanton, Jimmy, 86
Blue Five, 33
Blue Mariners, *98*
Bob Crosby Orchestra, The, *83*, 86
Bobcats, The, 86, 103
Bolden, Buddy, *8*, 9–11, 16
    home, *10*
Bolling, Claude, 141
Bose, Sterling, 51
Boswell, Connie, 75
Braslavasky, Pierre, 141
Breakdown, The, 65
Brown, Sandy, 154
Brown, Steve, 51

Brubeck, Dave, 123
    Take Five, 137
Brun, Philip, 72
Brunswick record label, 68
Bryce, Owen, 112
Buddy Bolden's Band, *9*
Buddy Petit's Jazz Band, *19*
Bunny Berigan's Band, 80
Burns, Tito, 144
Bush, Lennie, 132, *133*
Butterfield, Billy, 141
Byas, Don, 126
Byrd, Charlie, 137

Calloway, Cab, 82, *93*
Carey, Mutt, 108, *109*
Carlisle, Una Mae, 134
Carmichael, Hoagy, *30*
Carter, Benny, *94*, 96, 126
Carter, President Jimmy, *100*
Casa Loma Orchestra, 76, 77
Caton, Lauderic, 98
Cave Stompers, The, 141
Challis, Bill, 51, 53
Chisholm, George, 93
Christian, Charlie, 79
Christian, Emil, 60
Claes, Johnny, *98*
Clark, Kenny, 120, 154
Clayton, Buck, 147
Club Alabam Orchestra, *40*
Club Eleven, 132, *133*
Cole, Nat King, 100, *154*
Coleman, Bill, 72
Coleman, Ornette, 137
Coltrane, John, *136*, 137
Columbia Gramophone Company, 55
Columbia Records
    artists, signing up, 34
    first recordings, shelving, 26
Colyer, Ken, *142*, 143, 154
Combelle, Alix, 72
Condon, Eddie, 111
Cool jazz, 122
Cotton Club, The, 45, 84
Count Basie Band, 87
Crane River Jazz Band, *116*, 143
Crombie, Tony, 132, *133*, 144
Crosby, Bob, 103
Crump, Freddie, *98*
Curran, Dale, 129
Cutshall, Cutty, 111

Dance clubs, 85
Dance, Stanley, 147
Dankworth, Johnny, *130, 132, 133*, 144
Davis, Lew, *58*
Davis, Miles, *122*, 123–125
Davison, Wild Bill, 111, 141, 154
de Courville, Albert, 56
de Vries, Louis, 75, *75*
Decca record label, 104
Deitch, Gene, 129
Delaunay, Charles, 73, *74*, 75
Dodds, Johnny, 38, 107, 154

Dolphy, Eric, 137
Dominique, Natty, 104
Domnerus, Arne, 144
Donegal, Marquis of, *113*
Dorsey, Jimmy, 51, 71, 77, 84, 103, 154
Dorsey, Tommy, 38, 51, 77, 80, 84, 103, 124, 154
Duke Ellington and his Famous Orchestra, *52*, 68
Duke Ellington's Washingtonians, *43*
Dunn, Johnny, 36

Earl Hines' Grand Terrace Band, *51*
Eckstine, Billy, 125
Ehrling, Thore, 75
Ekyan, Andre, 72
Eldridge, Roy, 126
Elizalde, Fred, 68, *69*, 70
Ellington, Duke, 42, 53, *72*, 84, 86, 138, 154
    Britain, in, *90*, 91–93
Ericson, Rolf, 144
Esquire record label, 132
Evans, Gil, 123, *124*, 154
Ewans, Kai, 75

Fate Marable Band, *20*
Fawkes, Wally, *112*
Feather, Leonard, 129
Feldman, Victor, 99, *131*
Fenton, Bernie, 132
Firman, Bert, *66, 70*
Fitzgerald, Ella, *82*, 85, 86, 134, *135*, 141
Fletcher Henderson's Orchestra, 63, 77
Frank Coughlan's Dixielanders, 141
Frank Johnson's Fabulous Dixielanders, 141
Frankie Trumbauer's Orchestra, 68
Fred Elizalde and his Anglo-American Band, 69
Free-form, 137
French Quarter, The, 11

Garner, Erroll, *138*
Gennet Record Company
    advertisement from, *29*
    early recordings, 36, 38
    studios, *24, 36*, 38
George Lewis Band, The, 141
George Webb's Dixielanders, 112, *113*, 143
Geraldo, 95, *131*
Getz, Stan, 123, 126
    Desifinado, 137
Gillespie, Dizzy, *94*, 120, 125, 126, 129, *132*
Goldkette, Jean, *38, 47*, 51, 84
Goodman, Benny, 42, 46, 77, 79, *80*, 82, 84, 103, *124*, 154
Gordon, Dexter, *125*
Graeme Bell's Australian Jazz Band, *117*, 141
Granz, Norman, 125, 126
    Jazz at the Philharmonic, 127
Grappelli, Stephane, 72, *73*
Green, Charlie, 42
Gregor and his Gregorians, 72
Guy, Joe, 120

Hall, Edmund, *19*, 104, 154

Index

Hammersmith Palais, *57*
Hampton, Lionel, 79
Handy, WC, 34
Harris, Bill, 126
Harris, Jack, 95
Harris, Rex, 98, 115
Harry James Band, The, 80
Hawkins, Coleman, 42, 72, 86, 94, 96, 112, 116, 123, 126, *146*
Hayes, Tubby, 144, 154
Heard, JC, 126
Heath, Ted, *144, 145*
Henderson, Fletcher "Smack", 41, 42, 44, 63, 82, 84, 154
Herman, Woody, *81*, 124, 138, 154
Higginbotham, JC, 46
Hill, Bertha "Chippie", *35, 134*
Hill, Teddy, 94, 120
Hines, Earl, *51*, 75, 82
His Master's Voice, 55
Hodes, Art, *104*, 129
Holiday, Billie, *110*, 134, *135*, 141, 154
Hopkins, Ernest J., *27*
Hot Discography, 75
Hot Five, The, *35*, 41
Hughes, Spike, 68, 70, *70*
Humphrey Lyttelton and his Band, *113*
Hylton, Jack, 66, 95

Imperial record label, 63

Jack Hylton's Kit Kat Band, 66
Jackson, Edgar, *62, 63*, 65, 66
Jackson, Preston, 107
James, Harry, 46, 80, *83*, 84, 154
Jaspar, Bobby, 144
Jazz
    books on, 148–151
    criticism, 63, 65
    early reviews of, 26, 28, 30, 33, 34
    ephemera collections, 153
    Europe interpretations in, *54*, 55, 56
    films, 152
    first records, 26, 30
    future of, 156
    respectable, becoming, 100
    videos, 152
JAZZ FM, 149
Jazz Record, *105*
Jazz Writing, *104*
Jazzmen, 11
Jazzways, *103*
Jean Goldkette and his Orchestra, *47*, 53, 77
"Jelly Roll" Morton's Red Hot Peppers, *32*
Jig's Club, 98
Jitterbugs, 86
Johnny Dankworth Seven, The, *130*
Johnny Dunn and his Jazz Hounds, 36
Johnson, Bunk, *14*, *106*, 107, 108, 154
Johnson, JJ, 126
Jones, Max, *117*

Kaminsky, Max, 141
Keith Hounslow's Jazz Hounds, 141
Kennedy, President, 100
Kenton, Stan, 124, *124*, 125, 138, 154
Keppard, Freddie, *15*
Kid Ory's Creole Jazz Band, *24*, 25, 36
King Oliver and his Dixie Syncopaters, *42, 43*
King Oliver's Creole Jazz Band, 28, 36

Kirk, Andy, 82
Konitz, Lee, 123
Krahmer, Carlo, 132
Krupa, Gene, *79*, 80, *83*, 126, 154

Lacoume, Emile "Stalebread", *11, 154*
Ladnier, Tommy, 75, 104
Laine, Cleo, *135*
Lang, Eddie, 51, 60, 68
La Rocca, Nick, 58, 60
Lee, David, 149
Levaphone record label, 68
Levy's Record Shop, *68*
Lew Stone's Orchestra, *58*, 96
Lewis, George, 71, 107, 141, 154
Lewis, Ted, 71
London, Jazz Club, 143
Louisiana Five, the, 25
Luis Russell's Old Man River Orchestra, *45*
Lutcher, Nellie, 134
Luter, Claude, 141
Lyttelton, Humphrey, 32, *113, 114*, 115, 143, 145

Mahogany Hall, *8*
Mainstream jazz, 145, 147, 148
Manone, Wingy, 86, 103
Masman, Theo Uden, 75
McGarity, Lou, 111
McGhee, Howard, 126
McKinney, William, *50*
McKinney's Cotton Pickers, *50*
McPartland, Marion, 134
McRea, Carmen, 134, 141
Melly, George, *117, 144*
Melody Maker, *62*, 65, *89*
    advertisements, *67*
    "Gramophone Review", *70*
    No. 1 meetings, column on, 96
Melrose Brothers Music Company, *22*
Mertz, Paul, 38
Mezzrow, Milton "Mezz", *38*, 75, 104
Middleton, Velma, 75, *1*
Miff Mole and his Molers, *68*
Miles, Lizzie, *60, 61*
Miller, Glenn, *81*, 84
Mills Brothers, 93, *94*
Mingus, Charles, 100, 137, 154
Minton, Henry, 119
Modern jazz, 137
Modern Jazz Quartet, 123, *140*, 141
Mole, Miff, 25, *37*, 68, 111
Monk, Thelonious, 120, *121*
Morgan, Laurie, 132
Morgan, Sam, 27
Morris, Harry, 132
Morton, Ferdinand "Jelly Roll", 9, 16, *17, 31*, 66, *104*, 154
    ephemera, *30, 31*
    Red Hot Peppers, *32*, 63
Moten, Bennie, 49
Mound City Blue Blowers, *60*
Mrs Jack Hylton's Band, 94
Muddel, Joe, 132
Muggsy Spanier Ragtime Band, 104
    "Great 16, The", *105*
Mulligan, Gerry, 123, *131*, 141
Murphy, Rose, 134

Nat Gonella and his Georgians, 96
Neisen, Hank, 75

Nelson, "Big Eye" Louis, *14*
New Orleans, 9
    Canal Street, *8*
    capital of Louisiana, as, 14
    Mahogany Hall, *8*
    open-air entertainment, 15
    prostitutes, 16, 18, 20
    reputation, 16
    settlement of, 12
    United States, incorporated into, 12
New Orleans Blue Book, *13*
New Orleans Jazz – A Family Album, 20
New Orleans Owls, 26
New Orleans Rhythm Kings, *28, 36*, 38
Nicholas Albert, 45, 108
Nicholls, Horatio, 65
Nichols, Red, *37*
No. 1 Club, 96
Noone, Jimmy, 107, 154
Nunez, Yellow, 20, 25

OKEH label, 66, 68
Old Man River Orchestra, *45*
Oliver, King, 28, 29, 42, 154
Original Creole Jazz Band, 25
Original Creole Orchestra, *18*
Original Dixieland Jazz Band, *21*, 24, *56*
    contemporary cartoon of, *23*
    Creators of Jazz, as, 23
    England, playing in, 34, 55–58
    first records by, 15, 20, 26
Original Lyrical Five, The, *58*
Original Memphis Five, The, *24*, 25
Original New Orleans Band, 25
Oriole record label, 68
Ory, Kid, *10*, *24*, 42, *105*, 108, 154

Panassiè, Hughes, 73, 75, *75*
Papa Bue's Viking Jazz Band, 141
Parker, Charlie "Bird", 120, 125, 126, 154
    album covers, *118*
Parlophone record label, 68
Parry, Harry, *98*
Paul Specht's Canadian Club Orchestra, *61*
Paul Whiteman Band, The, *53*, 65
Payne, Jack, 95
Pepper, Art, 123, 154
Peterson, Oscar, 126, *147*
Petit, Buddy, *19*
Peyton, Benny, 59
Phillips, Flip, 126
Pickup, *104*
Pollack, Benny, 46, 51
Pollard, Tommy, 132, *133*
Polo, Danny, 51
Port Jackson Jazz Band, 141
Powell, Bud, 120
Prima, Louis, 103
Prince Charles, *101*
Pritchett, Gertrude, *134*
Pronk, Rob, 144

Quinquaginta Ramblers, 68
Quintette du Hot Club of France, 72, *73*, 93

Raeburn, Boyd, 124
Rainey, "Ma", *134*
Ramblers Band, 72, 94
Rank, Bill, 51
Ray Ventura's Collegians, 72
Record Changer, *128*, 129

Index

Record labels, 61
Record sleeves, *68*
Redman, Don, 82
Regal Novelty Orchestra, 61
Reinhardt, Django, 72, *73*, 93
Reliance Brass Band, *21*
Rena, Kid, *15*, 107
Rendell, Don, 144
Revival, the, 14, *102*, 104–117
Rewellioty, André, 141
Reys, Rita, 144
Rich, Buddy, 126, 138, 154
Rignold, Hugo, 65, 66
Riverboats, *18, 19*
Robey, Sir George, 56, 57
Rogers, Johnny, 132
Rollini, Adrian, 68
Rollins, Theodore "Sunny", 139
Ronnie Scott's Club, 144, 147
Roseland Ballroom, 41
Royal Orpheans, *74*
Rushing, Jimmy, 141
Russell, Luis, 13, *45*, 46

Sam Morgan's Jazz Band, *26*
Savoy Ballroom, Harlem, 85
Savoy Hotel, 68, *70*
Schilperoot, Peter, 141
Scott, Ronnie, 98, 132, *133*, 144
Scott, Shirley, 134
Service bands, 98
Sharon, Ralph, 144
Shaw, Artie, 82, *83*, 84, 103
Shaw, Hank, 132
Shearing, George, 123
Shorter, Wayne, 137
Sidney Bechet's Feetwarmers, 104
Sims, Zoot, 145, 154
Smith, Bessie, 134
Smith, Willie, 126
Snow, Valaida, 93, 134
Soho clubs, 96, 98

Soutar, John B., *65*
Southern Jazz Group, 141
Southern Syncopated Orchestra, *58, 59*, 60
Spanier, Muggsy, 46, 71, 104, 154
Spasm Band, 11
Specht, Paul, 60, *61*
Speed Webb and his Hollywood Red Devils, 48
Spike Hughes and his Decca-Dents, 68
Spikes' Seven Pods of Pepper, 25
Stein, John, *20*
Stewart, Rex, 141
Stone, Lew, *58*, 95
Storyville, 9
    closing, 18, 20
Superior Orchestra, The, *14*
Swing bands, 77–84
Swing College band, *141*
Swing Music, *93*
Swing record label, 72–75

Tatum, Art, *126*
Teagarden, Jack, 46
Ted Heath's Big Band, 144
Teddy Hill and his Orchestra, 94
ten Hoven, Boy, 75
Teschemacher, Frank, *38*
Thad Jones-Mel Lewis Orchestra, 138
Thatcher, Margaret, 100, *101*
Thielemans, Toots, 144
Trad jazz, 143
Tristano, Lenny, 123
Trumbauer, Frank, *47*, 51, 68

United Kingdom
    first bands playing in, 34, 55–58

Van Praag, Joost, 75
Vauchant, Leo, 72
Vaughan, Sarah, 125, 134, *135, 141*, 154
Ventura, Ray, 72
Venuti, Joe, 51, 68, 141

Victor Organisation
    Bluebird, 104
    first recordings, 26, 30
Vocalion Records, 42

Waller, Thomas "Fats", *86*, 93, 94, *154*
Washboard Serenaders, 93
Washington, Dinah, 134, *135*
Watters, Lu, 108
WC Handy and his Orchestra, 34
Webb, Chick, *82*, 84–86
Webb, George, 112
Webb, Speed, 48
Webster, Ben, *146*
Wells, Dickie, 72
Welsh, Alex, 143
White, Lulu, 9
Whiteman, Paul, 41, 53, 60, 65
Whiteway Jazz Band, 25
Whyte, Zack, *50*
Wilcox, Bert, *73*, 115
Wilcox, Stan, 115
Will Marion Cook's Southern Syncopated Orchestra, 60
Williams, Clarence, *33*
Williams, Mary Lou, 82, 134
Wilson, Garland, 96
Wilson, Teddy, 79, 141
Wolverine Orchestra, The, *29*, 38
    Riverboat Shuffle, 30
Woodland Band, The, *10*
Wright, Lawrence, 65

Yarra City Stompers, 141
Young, Lester, 122, 154

Zack Whyte and his Chocolate Beau Brummels, *50*

100 Club, 143

——ACKNOWLEDGEMENTS——

I wish to express my thanks to those who have helped me in the preparation of this volume, but 'thanks' is hardly the word to cover my heart-felt appreciation, especially to those who generously surrendered treasured memorabilia so that it may be included in these pages.

In this regard my especial thanks to Brian Davis for the programmes of concerts he attended after the ban on these appearing in Britain had been lifted in 1956. There are reminders of the joys that had been denied British jazz enthusiasts for over two decades.

Another special nod is to my dear friend, the erudite Alun Morgan who, over the hectic, often agonizing, six months I worked on this volume, was the almost daily recipient of my anxious enquiries which he readily answered.

More thanks: to Diana Heffer of the *Daily Telegraph* who rooted from that paper's archives the Court Circular relating to the appearance of Will Marion Cook's Southern Syncopated Orchestra featuring Sidney Bechet before King George V and Queen Mary at Buckingham Palace in 1919; to my fellow sufferer on tedious Indian Ocean convoys, Jimmy Brown, for supplying me with the photograph of the Blue Mariners, the band of the Royal Naval Patrol Service.

I have generally received assistance from so many that my very genuine fear is that I have omitted acknowledgement where it is due but, here, alphabetically— and with invidious special mentions here and there—is the listing of my friends:

Bruce Bastin, Dave Bennett, Bill Colyer, Bruce Crowther, Harold Davison (for permission to use the covers of the programme of concerts he promoted in the 1950s and 1960s), Gene Deitch (for his permission to reproduce his caricatures from the *Record Changer*), Diz Dizley (whose impressions of many visiting firemen graced Harold Davison's programmes), Geoff Ellison (for the material on the Club XI), Wally Fawkes (for his historic drawing of George Webb's Dixie-landers of which he was a founder member) and (across the stylistic fence) his impression of Ronnie Scott on the cover of the issue of *Jazz at Ronnie Scott's* commemorating, in October 1989, Scott's thirtieth anniversary as a club owner, Sandy Forbes, Bob Gardiner, Joe Green, Cindy Hacker, Mary Harris, Max Jones, Pete King (of Ronnie Scott's Club), Frank Liniger, Alf Lumby, Humphrey Lyttelton, Mike Pinfold, David Redfern, Brian Rust (who gave me the priceless photographs of Edgar Jackson taken before he entered the British jazz pantheon by becoming the first editor of the *Melody Maker*), Ray Smith of Ray's Jazz Shop (plus his helpful staff, Glyn Callingham, Mike Doyle and Bob Glass), John Whitehorn, and Al Woodrow.

This author is grateful for the support he received from designer, Mike Snell, who confronted with a mass of material of varying size and quality fashioned it into a coherent whole. Thanks, also, to John Wallace of Studio Editions, for patiently dealing with this apprehensive author's stream of queries and corrections, and to Liz Bacon, Maureen Lecoutre and Belinda Wilkinson on the staff of Studio Editions for their help.

I am indebted to Don Marquis, Curator, The Jazz Club Collections, Louisiana State University, New Orleans, and their staff photographer, Jan White Brantley for supplying prints of the Early New Orleans Band's appearing in Chapter One.

My thanks to the publishers and editors of the following magazines for permission to reproduce the covers of their magazines: Peter Boizot and editor Melissa Swanson of *Jazz Express*; Bert Wilcox of *Jazz Illustrated*; Eddie Cook of *Jazz Journal*; Max Jones of *Jazz Music*; Art Hodes of *Jazz Record*; Ronnie Scott and Pete King of *Jazz at Ronnie Scott's*; IPC Magazines and editor Alan Jones of the *Melody Maker*; Maurice Kinn of the *New Musical Express* and *Observer Publications*; and Tony Russell of *Jazz FM*.

Additional thanks to Laurie Wright for permission to print extracts from articles in *Storyville*, and to reproduce the vintage labels that appeared in that journal and in *King Joe Oliver* by Walter Allen and Brian Ruse, recently updated by Laurie Wright.

Thanks to the various record companies for permission to reproduce their record labels/album sleeves; Decca, HMV, Parlophone, Regal, Columbia, BBC Records, Vogue, BMG, Esquire, Harlequin, Hep, EMI, and Affinity.

Thanks to Warner Bros. for use of the publicity brochure for *Bird* directed by Clint Eastwood, and to Hendring Videos for permission to use the covers of their jazz videos.

The following publishers kindly gave permission for certain book covers to be reproduced: Macmillan, Quartet, Observer Books, Albert Knopf, Greenberg, Storyville Books, Thames and Hudson, Spring Books, Elm Tree Books, Bloomsbury Books, David and Charles, Michael Joseph, Studio Vista, Cassell, Orbis, Blandford Press and Thomas Crowell.

Again, many, many thanks to all.

Jim Godbolt
London, May 1990